The best of Mrs Beeton's Christmas

The best of Mrs Beeton's Christmas

WEIDENFELD & NICOLSON

This edition produced for The Book People Ltd, Hall Wood Avenue, Haydock, St Helens WA11 9UL

First published in 2006 by the Orion Publishing Group Ltd
5 Upper St Martin's Lane
London
WC2H 9EA

Designed by seagulls and cbdesign
Index prepared by Chris Bell
Produced by Omnipress Ltd, Eastbourne
Printed in China

Contents

Soups and Stocks 1
Starters and Snacks 21
Poultry and Game 39
Meat Dishes 71
Fish Dishes 91
Vegetarian Main Courses 99
Side Dishes 105
Stuffings 129
Savoury Sauces 141
Puddings and Desserts 155
Sweet Sauces and Butters 185
Cakes and Baking 197
Beverages 223
Table Laying, Menu Planning and Christmas Countdown 231
Useful Weights and Measures 242
Index 245

Soups & Stocks

Hearty, warming soups make convenient meals-in-a-bowl at this busy time of year, based on stocks that utilise your leftovers and peelings. Serve soup as a light festive starter using seasonal ingredients, garnished with cream, herbs, toasted nuts or croutons.

BORSCH

The vivid colour of this soup makes it an ideal festive starter.

30 ml / 2 tbsp oil
1 onion, roughly chopped
1 garlic clove, sliced
1 carrot, sliced
1 turnip, sliced
1 swede, sliced
2 tomatoes, peeled and chopped
350 g / 12 oz raw beetroot, grated
1 bay leaf
2 litres / 3½ pints Rich Strong Stock (page 16)
30 ml / 2 tbsp tomato purée
salt and pepper
225 g / 8 oz cabbage, sliced
225 g / 8 oz potatoes, cubed
5 ml / 1 tsp cider vinegar
150 ml / ¼ pint soured cream
chopped dill, to garnish

Heat the oil in a large saucepan. Add the onion, garlic, carrot, turnip and swede and cook for 10 minutes, stirring frequently to prevent the vegetables from sticking to the base of the pan. Stir in the tomatoes and beetroot with the bay leaf. Add the stock and tomato purée, with salt and pepper to taste. Bring to the boil, lower the heat, cover and simmer for 1 hour.

Add the sliced cabbage and cubed potato. Stir in the vinegar and simmer for 15 minutes more or until the potato cubes are tender. Taste the soup and add more salt and pepper, if required.

Leave to stand for 5 minutes. Serve topped with soured cream and garnished with dill.

SERVES SIX

CHESTNUT SOUP

Chestnuts have a robust flavour which combines well with beef stock in this unusual soup.

350 g / 12 oz chestnuts
1.4 litres / 2½ pints Rich Strong Stock (page 16) or Vegetable Stock (page 20)
salt and cayenne pepper
2.5 ml / ½ tsp ground mace
150 ml / ¼ pint single cream

Make a small slit in the shell of each chestnut. Place the chestnuts in a saucepan of boiling water and cook for 5 minutes. Drain, carefully removing the shells and skins while the chestnuts are still very hot.

Put the peeled chestnuts into a pan and cover with 400 ml / 14 fl oz of the stock. Bring to the boil, lower the heat and simmer for 30–40 minutes or until the chestnuts break when touched with a fork. Drain the chestnuts thoroughly, reserving about 250 ml / 9 fl oz of the chestnut-flavoured stock.

Rub the chestnuts through a sieve into a clean pan. Stir in the remaining stock, with enough of the chestnut-flavoured stock to give a good flavour (see Mrs Beeton's Tip). Add salt, cayenne and mace to taste.

Bring the soup to just below boiling point, stirring frequently, then remove from the heat and stir in the cream. Serve at once.

SERVES FOUR TO SIX

MRS BEETON'S TIP

The stock in which the chestnuts have been cooked will have a sweetish flavour which may not be to everyone's taste, so add it with discretion.

JERUSALEM ARTICHOKE SOUP

Unlike the globe artichoke, which grows above the ground, the Jerusalem artichoke is a tuber. It makes a delicious winter soup.

45 g / 1½ oz butter
3 rindless back bacon slices, chopped
4 celery sticks, thinly sliced
1 small turnip, cubed
1 onion, chopped
1 kg / 2¼ lb Jerusalem artichokes (see Mrs Beeton's Tip)
1.5 litres / 2¾ pints White Stock (page 18)
salt and pepper
cayenne pepper
300 ml / ½ pint double cream

Melt the butter in a large saucepan. Add the bacon, celery, turnip and onion and fry over gentle heat for about 10 minutes until the vegetables are soft but not coloured.

Peel and cube the artichokes. Add them to the pan with the stock. Bring to the boil, lower the heat and simmer for about 15 minutes or until all the vegetables are tender.

Purée the soup in a blender or food processor, or rub through a sieve into a clean pan. Add salt, pepper and cayenne to taste. Stir in the cream and reheat gently. Do not allow the soup to boil after adding the cream.

SERVES SIX

MRS BEETON'S TIP

The flesh of Jerusalem artichokes discolours very rapidly, so prepare the vegetables only when required or put the cubes into water to which a little lemon juice or wine vinegar has been added.

PARSNIP SOUP

25 g / 1 oz butter
1 onion, chopped
450 g / 1 lb parsnips, sliced
1 litre / 1¾ pints Chicken Stock (page 18)
or Vegetable Stock (page 20)
salt and cayenne pepper
150 ml / ¼ pint single cream
30 ml / 2 tbsp pine nuts, to garnish (optional)

Melt the butter in a large saucepan, add the onion and parsnips, and cook over gentle heat for 10 minutes, turning frequently to coat them in the butter.

Add the stock, with salt and cayenne pepper to taste. Bring to the boil, lower the heat and simmer for 20 minutes until the parsnips are very soft.

Purée the soup in a blender or food processor, or rub through a sieve into a clean pan. Reheat it to just below boiling point, then stir in most of the cream, reserving about 30 ml / 2 tbsp for the garnish.

Meanwhile spread out the pine nuts (if used) in a grill pan and toast them under a hot grill until golden. Ladle the soup into individual bowls and top each portion with a swirl of cream and a sprinkling of toasted pine nuts.

SERVES FOUR

VARIATION

- **Spiced Parsnip Soup** Add 5 ml / 1 tsp good-quality curry powder to the onion and parsnips when cooking in the butter. Substitute plain yogurt for the cream and use roughly chopped cashew nuts instead of the pine nuts. Sprinkle with a little chopped fresh coriander leaves, if liked.

CABBAGE SOUP

Cabbage and bacon go wonderfully well together, a fact that is celebrated in this hearty soup.

15 ml / 1 tbsp oil
175 g / 6 oz rindless streaky bacon rashers
2 carrots, thinly sliced
1 large onion, thinly sliced
1 large cabbage, shredded
1.1 litres / 2 pints White Stock (page 18)
pepper to taste
croutons, to garnish (optional)

Heat the oil in a large heavy-bottomed saucepan or flameproof casserole. Add the bacon and cook, stirring, for 5 minutes. Add the carrots and onion, then cook gently for 10 minutes. Stir in the cabbage and add the stock. Bring to the boil, lower the heat and cover the pan. Simmer for 45 minutes, until the vegetables are tender and the soup well flavoured.

Taste the soup for seasoning and add pepper. The bacon usually makes the soup sufficiently salty, depending on the stock. Skim off any excess surface fat, then serve the soup very hot, with croutons, if liked.

SERVES EIGHT

CARROT SOUP

Grating the vegetables speeds up the cooking time, making this an ideal soup for those occasions when time is short.

600 ml / 1 pint Chicken Stock (page 18), or Vegetable Stock (page 20)
3 carrots, grated
1 onion, finely chopped
1 potato, grated
25 g / 1 oz butter
25 g / 1 oz plain flour
300 ml / ½ pint milk
salt and pepper
grated nutmeg

Combine the stock, carrots, onion and potato in a saucepan. Bring to the boil, lower the heat and simmer gently for about 15 minutes, or until the vegetables are tender.

Meanwhile melt the butter in a separate saucepan, add the flour and cook for 1 minute. Gradually stir in the milk, then add the stock and vegetables. Heat, stirring constantly, until the mixture boils and thickens. Add salt, pepper and nutmeg to taste. Serve at once, with triangles of hot toast, if liked.

SERVES FOUR

VARIATION

- **Carrot and Orange Soup** Cut the carrot into matchstick strips and use 1 parsnip, cut into similar strips, instead of the potato. Use 900 ml / 1½ pints stock and add 60 ml / 4 tbsp fresh orange juice. Omit the milk and do not thicken the soup.

BEAN SOUP

The perfect warmer for a chilly winter's night, this soup is a meal in itself.

450 g / 1 lb haricot beans, soaked overnight in water to cover
100 g / 4 oz fat bacon, diced
2 onions, sliced
10 ml / 2 tsp dried thyme
salt and pepper
15 ml / 1 tbsp chopped parsley

Drain the beans. Put them in a large heavy-bottomed saucepan. Add 2.25 litres / 4 pints water and bring to the boil. Boil vigorously for 10 minutes, then lower the heat and simmer for 45 minutes or until the beans are almost tender. Drain, reserving the bean stock.

Put the bacon in the clean pan and heat gently until the fat runs. Add the onions and fry over moderate heat for 3–4 minutes. Stir in the beans with the thyme. Add the reserved bean stock, with salt and pepper to taste. Simmer for 1 hour, stirring occasionally to prevent the soup from sticking to the pan.

Check the seasoning and add more salt and pepper if required. Stir in the parsley and serve at once, with chunks of wholemeal bread.

SERVES SIX TO EIGHT

VARIATIONS

- **Two-Bean Soup** Use half red kidney beans instead of haricot beans alone. Add 1 diced green pepper with the onions.
- **Vegetarian Bean Soup** Omit the bacon and fry the onion in 25 g / 1 oz butter with 1 crushed garlic clove. Stir in 45 ml / 3 tbsp tahini with the parsley.

CAULIFLOWER SOUP

1 large cauliflower
25 g / 1 oz butter
1 onion, finely chopped
900 ml / 1½ pints milk
salt and pepper
2 egg yolks
150 ml / ¼ pint single cream
50 g / 2 oz toasted flaked almonds, to garnish

Steam the cauliflower whole for 20–30 minutes until tender. Cut it into florets, reserving any leaves or tender stem.

Melt the butter in a small frying pan. Add the onion and cook over gentle heat for about 10 minutes, until soft but not coloured. Purée the cauliflower and the onion mixture with 250 ml / 9 fl oz of the milk in a blender or food processor, then rub through a fine sieve into a clean pan.

Stir the remaining milk into the pan, with salt and pepper to taste. Heat the soup to just below boiling point, then lower the heat so that it barely simmers. In a small bowl, mix the egg yolks with the cream. Stir a little of the hot soup into the egg mixture, mix well, then add the contents of the bowl to the soup, stirring over low heat until it thickens. Serve at once, topped with toasted almonds.

SERVES FOUR

MRS BEETON'S TIP

To make a quick cauliflower soup, break the vegetable into florets and place in a saucepan with 1 diced potato and 1 chopped onion. Add 600 ml / 1 pint chicken stock and bring to the boil. Simmer, covered for 30 minutes, then purée. Add 300 ml / ½ pint milk and seasoning to taste. Heat without boiling.

YELLOW SPLIT PEA SOUP

30 ml / 2 tbsp oil
6 rindless streaky bacon rashers, chopped
1 large onion, finely chopped
100 g / 4 oz yellow split peas, soaked overnight in water to cover
2 litres / 3½ pints Chicken Stock (page 18) or Vegetable Stock (page 20)
60 ml / 4 tbsp chopped celery leaves
2 parsley sprigs
2 bay leaves
5 ml / 1 tsp chopped summer savory or 2.5 ml / ½ tsp dried savory
salt and pepper

Heat the oil in a large saucepan. Add the bacon and onion and fry for 10 minutes over gentle heat, until the onion is soft but not coloured.

Drain the split peas and add them to the pan with the stock, celery leaves, parsley, bay leaves and savory. Add salt and pepper to taste. Bring to the boil, lower the heat and simmer for about 2 hours, or until the peas are very tender. If the soup becomes too thick, add water or extra stock.

Remove the parsley sprigs and bay leaves. Serve the soup as it is, or purée in a blender or food processor. Alternatively, rub through a sieve into a clean pan. Reheat, stirring frequently to prevent the soup from sticking to the pan, and serve at once.

SERVES FOUR TO SIX

VARIATION

- **Pea and Ham Soup** Save the stock when boiling a joint of ham or bacon as it makes delicious split pea soup. Omit the streaky bacon and do not add seasoning until the soup is cooked.

PRESSURE COOKER TIP

It is not necessary to soak the split peas if the soup is to be made in a pressure cooker. Fry the bacon and onion in the oil in the open cooker. Add the split peas and herbs as in the recipe above, but reduce the amount of stock to 1 litre / 1¾ pints. Put the lid on the cooker and bring to 15 lb pressure. Cook for 12 minutes. Reduce pressure slowly, then continue as described above, adding more stock to adjust the consistency as desired.

BAKED SOUP

It isn't always convenient to make soup on top of the cooker. This simple solution – a soup baked in the oven – dates from Victorian times.

450 g / 1 lb lean boneless stewing beef or lamb, cubed
2 onions, finely sliced
2 carrots, finely sliced
25 g / 1 oz long-grain rice
225 g / 8 oz split peas
salt and pepper

Preheat the oven to 150°C / 300°F / gas 2. Combine all the ingredients in a large flameproof casserole. Add 1.25 litres / 2½ pints water.

Bring to the boil, cover tightly and transfer to the oven. Bake for 3½–4 hours. Taste the soup and add more salt and pepper if necessary. Skim off surface fat and serve.

SERVES SIX TO EIGHT

SMOKED HADDOCK CHOWDER

450 g / 1 lb smoked haddock fillet, skinned
750 ml / 1¼ pints milk
50 g / 2 oz butter
1 small onion, finely chopped
100 g / 4 oz mushrooms, finely chopped
40 g / 1½ oz plain flour
250 ml / 9 fl oz single cream
freshly ground black pepper

Put the haddock fillets into a saucepan with the milk and heat to simmering point. Simmer for about 10 minutes until just tender. Drain the fish, reserving the cooking liquid, remove the skin and shred the fish lightly.

Melt the butter in a clean pan, add the onion and mushrooms and fry gently for about 10 minutes until soft. Do not allow the onion to colour.

Stir in the flour and cook for 1 minute, stirring constantly. Gradually add the fish-flavoured milk, stirring until smooth. Bring to the boil, lower the heat and simmer until thickened.

Off the heat, add the cream and the shredded haddock. Return the pan to the heat and warm through gently. Do not allow the soup to boil after adding the cream. Top with a generous grinding of black pepper and serve at once.

SERVES FOUR TO SIX

TURKEY SOUP

carcass and trimmings of 1 turkey
25 g / 1 oz lean back bacon rashers, rinds removed
25 g / 1 oz butter
1 onion, sliced
1 large carrot, sliced
½ parsnip, sliced
25 g / 1 oz plain flour
1 litre / 1¾ pints water for each 400 g / 14 oz cooked turkey leftovers
bouquet garni
1 clove
25–50 g / 1–2 oz breast of turkey
salt and pepper

Weigh the carcass and trimmings, and break the carcass into pieces. Dice the bacon. Melt the butter in a large saucepan. Add the carcass pieces, meat trimmings and bacon and fry until browned. Remove them and reserve the fat in the pan. Put the vegetables into the pan and fry gently until golden brown. Stir in the water and heat to boiling point. Add the bouquet garni and clove. Return the turkey carcass, trimmings and bacon to the pan. Cover and simmer for 1½–2 hours.

Meanwhile, cut the pieces of breast meat into 5 mm / ¼ in dice. Strain the soup, add the diced meat and reheat. Season to taste.

SERVES FOUR

MRS BEETON'S TIP

Leftover pieces of stuffing improve the flavour and help to thicken the soup.

COCK-A-LEEKIE

100 g / 4 oz prunes
450 g / 1 lb leeks, trimmed, sliced and washed
1 x 1.4 kg / 3 lb chicken
3 rindless streaky bacon rashers, chopped
2.5 ml / ½ tsp salt
1 bouquet garni
1.25 ml / ¼ tsp pepper

Soak the prunes overnight in a small bowl of water, then drain them and remove the stones. Set aside, with about one-third of the drained leek slices.

Put the chicken, with its giblets if available, and bacon in a deep saucepan. Add cold water to cover (about 2 litres / 3½ pints). Stir in the salt and bring slowly to simmering point.

Add the remaining leeks to the pan, with the bouquet garni and pepper. Cover, then simmer gently for about 3 hours or until the chicken is cooked through and tender.

Carefully remove the chicken, discard the skin, then carve off the meat and cut it into fairly large serving pieces. Return the chicken meat to the soup and add the reserved prunes and leeks. Simmer gently for about 30 minutes, until the prunes are cooked but not broken. Skim off surface fat and check seasoning before serving.

SERVES SIX TO EIGHT

MRS BEETON'S TIP

Ready-to-eat dried prunes may be used. There is no need to presoak them.

SCOTCH BROTH

This economical soup was originally intended to furnish two meals: the meat was removed after cooking and served separately. Today it is more usual to cut up the meat and add it to the soup.

25 g / 1 oz pearl barley
450 g / 1 lb middle neck of lamb, trimmed of excess fat
1.4 litres / 2½ pints White Stock or Chicken Stock (page 18)
1 onion, chopped
1 leek, trimmed, sliced and washed
2 carrots, sliced
1 swede, cubed
salt and pepper

Put the barley in a small saucepan with water to cover. Bring to the boil, then drain off the water and transfer the barley to a large pan with the meat and stock. Bring the mixture to the boil, skim off any scum on the surface, then lower the heat and simmer gently for 2 hours.

Add all the vegetables with plenty of salt and pepper. Simmer for a further 45–60 minutes. Lift out the meat, remove it from the bones, and roughly chop it. Skim off any fat from the broth, add more salt and pepper if required, then replace the chopped meat. Serve very hot.

SERVES FOUR

PRESSURE COOKER TIP

It is not necessary to blanch the barley. Simply combine the ingredients in the cooker, reducing the amount of stock to 900 ml / 1½ pints. The cooker should not be more than half full. Put the lid on, bring to 15 lb pressure and cook for 10 minutes. Reduce the pressure slowly. Continue as above.

RICH STRONG STOCK

This recipe makes a large quantity of stock which freezes well for future use. Although the quantities may be reduced, a large volume of liquid is required to cover marrow bones. It is more practical to invest in a large stockpot or saucepan and to boil a large quantity occasionally than to reduce the weight of ingredients in proportion to water to make a weaker meat stock.

675 g / 1½ lb shin of beef on the bone
675 g / 1½ lb knuckle of veal on the bone, or other stewing veal
450 g / 1 lb beef marrow bones
1 chicken drumstick or poultry trimmings
1 onion, sliced
1 carrot, quartered
100 g / 4 oz gammon or bacon, diced
1 small turnip, roughly chopped
2 celery sticks, quartered
2 open cup mushrooms, quartered
1 tomato, quartered
1 bouquet garni
4 white peppercorns
2 cloves
1 blade of mace

Set the oven at 200°C / 400°F / gas 6. Put the bones in a roasting tin and roast for about 2 hours until browned. Transfer the bones to a large saucepan. Pour off the fat from the tin, add some boiling water and stir to scrape all the sediment off the tin. Then add to the bones in the pan. Add the onion and carrot.

Add about 5.6 litres / 10 pints water to cover the bones generously. Bring to the boil, skim the surface, then lower the heat and add the remaining ingredients. Simmer for about 5 hours. Cool, then strain. Skim off surface fat. Season and use as required.

MAKES ABOUT 5.6 litres / 10 pints

CLARIFYING STOCK

Scald a saucepan (not aluminium), a piece of muslin, a metal sieve and a whisk. Pour the strained stock into the pan. Lightly whisk 2 egg whites and crush the shells from 2 eggs; add to the stock. Heat slowly to simmering point, whisking to form a thick white crust. Stop whisking, allow the stock to rise in the pan, then turn the heat off just before it boils. Repeat twice more. Line the sieve with the muslin and place it over a clean bowl. Strain the stock through the muslin. Try not to break the crust which acts as a filter.

PRESSURE COOKER TIP

Meat and poultry stocks, made with raw or cooked meat and bones, can be prepared in the pressure cooker in approximately 40 minutes at 15 lb pressure. Follow the manufacturer's recommendations regarding the maximum quantity of ingredients and liquid for the pan; failing this, make a concentrated stock by reducing the volume of water to ensure that the pan is no more than half to two-thirds full. Add extra water and simmer briefly in the open pan after the pressure has been reduced.

WHITE STOCK

1.4 kg / 3 lb knuckle of veal on the bone, or other stewing veal
2 chicken drumsticks or poultry trimmings
1 onion, sliced
1 carrot, quartered
2 celery sticks, quartered
2 open cup mushrooms, quartered
1 bouquet garni
4 white peppercorns
1 blade of mace

Put the bones in a large saucepan. Add 900 ml / 1½ pints water. Bring to the boil, skim the surface, then add the remaining ingredients. Lower the heat and simmer for 30 minutes. Add a further 900 ml / 1½ pints water and simmer for about 3 hours more. Cool quickly, then strain. Skim off surface fat. Season and use as required.

MAKES ABOUT 1.5 litres / 2¾ pints

CHICKEN STOCK

4 chicken drumsticks or 1 meaty chicken carcass
1 small onion, sliced
1 carrot, roughly chopped
1 celery stick, sliced
1 bouquet garni
5 ml / 1 tsp white peppercorns

Break or chop the carcass into manageable pieces. Put it in a large saucepan with 1.75 litres / 3 pints cold water. Bring to the boil; skim the surface. Add the remaining ingredients, lower the heat and simmer for 3–4 hours. Cool quickly, then strain. Skim off surface fat. Season and use as required.

MAKES ABOUT 1.4 litres / 2½ pints

VARIATION

- **Rich Chicken Stock** Use drumsticks and roast them at 200°C / 400°F / gas 6 for 40 minutes. Drain off the fat. Continue as above, adding 225 g / 8 oz cubed belly pork with the chicken.
- **Game Stock** Use the carcasses of 1 or 2 game birds such as pheasant or grouse, with the giblets, instead of the chicken.

FISH STOCK

fish bones and trimmings without gills, which cause bitterness
5 ml / 1 tsp salt
1 small onion, sliced
2 celery sticks, sliced
4 white peppercorns
1 bouquet garni

Break up any bones and wash the fish trimmings, if used. Put the bones, trimmings or heads in a saucepan and cover with 1 litre / 1¾ pints cold water. Add the salt.

Bring the liquid to the boil and add the vegetables, peppercorns and bouquet garni. Lower the heat, cover and simmer gently for 30–40 minutes. Do not cook the stock for longer than 40 minutes or it may develop a bitter taste. Strain, cool quickly and use as required.

MAKES ABOUT 1 litre / 1¾ pints

VARIATION

- **White Wine Fish Stock** Add 100 ml / 3½ fl oz dry white wine, 4–5 mushroom stalks and 1 sliced carrot. Simmer for 30 minutes only.

VEGETABLE STOCK

Vary the vegetables according to the market selection and your personal taste.

2 onions, sliced
2 leeks, trimmed, sliced and washed
1 small turnip, chopped
4 celery sticks, sliced
2 tomatoes, chopped
1 bouquet garni
6 black peppercorns
2 cloves
a few lettuce leaves
a few spinach leaves
a few watercress sprigs
2.5 ml / ½ tsp yeast extract (optional)
salt

Put the root vegetables, celery, tomatoes, herbs and spices in a large saucepan. Pour in 2 litres / 3½ pints water. Bring to the boil, lower the heat and simmer for 1 hour.

Add the lettuce, spinach and watercress and simmer for 1 hour more. Stir in the yeast extract, if using, and add salt to taste.

MAKES ABOUT 1.75 litres / 3 pints

Starters & Snacks

Make rich meat and fish pâtés, celebratory salmon and seafood bites, spiced nuts and cheese pastries for drinks parties, or potted delicacies perfect for impromptu lunches and last-minute gifts.

POTTED SALMON

450 g / 1 lb cold cooked salmon, skinned and boned
salt and pepper
pinch of cayenne pepper
pinch of ground mace
anchovy essence
50 g / 2 oz softened clarified butter, plus extra for sealing (see Mrs Beeton's Tip, page 23)

Pound the salmon flesh in a mortar or process roughly in a blender or food processor. Add salt, pepper, cayenne, mace and anchovy essence to taste. Blend in the softened clarified butter thoroughly.

Rub the mixture through a fine sieve into a bowl. Turn into small pots. Cover with a layer of clarified butter and refrigerate until the butter is firm.

MAKES ABOUT 450 g /1 lb

POTTED SHRIMPS OR PRAWNS

225 g/ 8 oz unsalted butter
450 g / 1 lb peeled cooked shrimps or prawns (small brown shrimps have a particularly good flavour)
1.25 ml / ¼ tsp ground white pepper
1.25 ml / ¼ ground mace
1.25 ml / ¼ ground cloves
dill sprigs, to garnish

Melt the butter in a saucepan, add the shrimps or prawns and heat very gently, without boiling. Add the pepper, mace and cloves.

Using a slotted spoon, transfer the shrimps or prawns to small pots. Pour a little of the hot spiced butter into each pot.

Set the remaining spiced butter aside until the residue has settled, then pour over the shrimps or prawns. Chill until the butter is firm. Store in a refrigerator for no more than 48 hours. Garnish with dill.

MAKES ABOUT 675 g / 1½ lb

POTTED HAM

butter for greasing
1.25 kg / 2¾ lb cooked ham, not too lean
1.25 ml / ¼ tsp ground mace
1.25 ml / ¼ tsp grated nutmeg
pinch of cayenne pepper
1.25 ml / ¼ tsp ground black pepper
melted clarified butter (see Mrs Beeton's Tip)

Grease a pie dish. Set the oven at 180°C / 350°F / gas 4. Mince the ham two or three times, then pound well and rub through a fine sieve into a clean bowl. Add the spices and peppers and mix well. Spoon the ham mixture into the prepared dish, cover with buttered greaseproof paper and bake for about 45 minutes.

When cooked, allow to cool, then turn into small pots and cover with clarified butter. Refrigerate until the butter is firm.

MAKES ABOUT 1 kg / 2¼ lb

MRS BEETON'S TIP

To clarify butter, heat gently until melted, then stand for 2–3 minutes. Carefully pour the clear yellow liquid on top into a clean bowl, leaving the residue behind. This is the clarified butter.

POTTED VENISON

100–150 g / 4–5 oz butter
1 kg / 2¼ lb cooked venison, finely minced
60 ml / 4 tbsp port or stock
1.25 ml / ¼ tsp grated nutmeg
1.25 ml / ¼ tsp ground allspice
salt
2.5 ml / ½ tsp freshly ground black pepper
melted clarified butter (see Mrs Beeton's Tip, page 23)

Melt 100 g / 4 oz of the butter in a saucepan. Add the minced venison, port or stock, spices, salt and pepper. If the meat is very dry, add the remaining butter.

Cook the mixture gently until blended and thoroughly hot. Immediately, turn into small pots and leave to cool. Cover with clarified butter. When cool, refrigerate until the butter is firm.

MAKES ABOUT 1 kg / 2¼ lb

POTTED BEEF

A popular Victorian dish, potted beef will keep for up to a week in the refrigerator when made from very fresh meat and sealed with clarified butter. Chuck and skirt steak are both ideal cuts to use.

butter for greasing
450 g / 1 lb lean braising steak, trimmed and cubed
blade of mace
pinch of ground ginger
30 ml / 2 tbsp beef stock
75 g / 3 oz butter
salt and pepper
melted clarified butter (see Mrs Beeton's Tip, page 23)

Set the oven at 150°C / 300°F/ gas 2. Combine the beef cubes, mace, ginger and stock in a casserole or ovenproof dish. Cover tightly with buttered greaseproof paper and foil.

Bake for 3½–4 hours, until the meat is very tender. Remove the mace. Mince the meat twice, then pound it well with the butter and any meat juices remaining in the casserole to make a smooth paste. Add salt and pepper to taste.

Turn into small pots and cover with clarified butter. When cool, refrigerate the potted beef until the butter is firm.

MAKES ABOUT 450 G / 1 LB

POTTED GAME

A small amount of game, potted with cooked ham or bacon, makes a satisfying starter.

350 g / 12 oz cooked boneless game meat, trimmed
100 g / 4 oz cooked ham or boiled bacon, trimmed
75 g / 3 oz butter, softened
pinch of cayenne pepper
salt
1.25 ml / ¼ tsp ground black pepper
melted clarified butter (see Mrs Beeton's Tip, page 23)
bay leaves and juniper berries, to garnish

Mince the game and ham or bacon very finely. Pound it to a smooth paste, gradually working in the butter. Alternatively, grind the meats in a food processor; add the butter and process briefly to combine. Mix in the cayenne, with salt and pepper to taste.

Turn the mixture into small pots and cover with clarified butter. Refrigerate the pots until the butter is firm. Garnish and serve.

MAKES ABOUT 450 g / 1 lb

SMOKED MACKEREL PÂTÉ

25 g / 1 oz clarified butter, plus extra for sealing
(see Mrs Beeton's Tip, page 23)
2 shallots, finely chopped
75 g / 3 oz tomato purée
5 ml / 1 tsp soft light brown sugar
juice of ½ lemon
8 crushed peppercorns
15 ml / 1 tbsp shredded fresh basil
1.25 ml / ¼ tsp dried tarragon
few drops of Tabasco sauce
450 g / 1 lb smoked mackerel fillets, skinned
75 ml / 5 tbsp double cream

Melt the clarified butter in a saucepan, add the shallots and cook over gentle heat for 2–3 minutes until soft. Add the tomato purée, sugar, lemon juice, peppercorns and herbs and cook gently for 4–5 minutes. Stir in the Tabasco sauce, then set aside to cool.

Roughly purée the shallot mixture, mackerel fillets and cream in a blender or food processor. Turn into a suitable dish or mould and cool. Cover with clarified butter and chill until firm. Serve with toast.

MAKES ABOUT 450 g / 1 lb

HERRING ROE PÂTÉ

100 g / 4 oz soft herring roes
salt and pepper
75 g / 3 oz butter
30 ml / 2 tbsp, lemon juice
15 ml / 1 tbsp chopped parsley
chopped lettuce, to garnish

Sprinkle the herring roes with salt and pepper. Melt 25 g / 1 oz of the butter in a small frying pan, add the roes and fry gently for 10 minutes. Process the roes to a smooth paste in a blender or food processor, or pound them in a mortar.

Soften the remaining butter and add it to the roe mixture, with the lemon juice and parsley. Turn into a small mould and chill for 2 hours until set.

Turn out of the mould, garnish with the chopped lettuce and serve with fingers of hot dry toast or fresh brown bread.

MAKES ABOUT 175 g / 6 oz

VARIATION

- **Herbed Herring Roe Pâté** Use 30 ml / 2 tbsp chopped fresh dill instead of the parsley and add 15 ml / 1 tbsp snipped chives.
- **Herring Roe and Prawn Pâté** Prepare the pâté as above. Roughly chop 100 g / 4 oz peeled cooked prawns and add them to the pâté before putting in the mould. Garnish with whole cooked prawns, if liked.
- **Herring Roe Sauce** Cook the herring as in the recipe above, frying 30 ml / 2 tbsp finely chopped onion in the butter before adding the roes. Process to a paste, tip into a saucepan and add 250 ml / 9 fl oz double cream. Season to taste with salt, pepper and lemon juice. Serve with grilled white fish, garnished with a few peeled cooked prawns for colour.

LIVER PÂTÉ

Serve this flavoursome pâté in the dish in which it was cooked, with hot dry toast, or cut into slices and serve with salad.

butter for greasing
75 g / 3 oz butter
100 g / 4 oz lean rindless bacon rashers, chopped
225 g / 8 oz calf's or pig's liver, trimmed and chopped
225 g / 8 oz chicken livers, trimmed and chopped
1 small onion, finely chopped
a few gherkins, chopped (optional)
1–2 hard-boiled eggs. chopped
salt and pepper
5–10 ml / 1–2 tsp dried mixed herbs
melted clarified butter (see Mrs Beeton's Tip, page 23)

Grease an ovenproof terrine or similar dish. Set the oven at 180°C / 350°F / gas 4. Melt the butter in a frying pan, add the bacon, livers and onion and fry gently for 5–6 minutes. Mince finely twice or process in a blender or food processor to a smooth paste. Add the chopped gherkins and hard-boiled eggs, with salt, pepper and herbs to taste. Stir well. Spoon into the prepared dish; cover with buttered greaseproof paper.

Stand the dish in a roasting tin and add enough hot water to come to within 2.5 cm / 1 inch of the rim of the tin. Bake for 30 minutes.

When cooked, cover immediately with a layer of clarified butter. Leave to cool, then chill before serving. Alternatively, place under a light weight and cover with clarified butter when cold.

MAKES ABOUT 675 g / 1½ lb

STORAGE AND USAGE

Always keep pâté and potted foods covered on a low shelf in the refrigerator. Remove slices or portions as required and return the rest to the refrigerator promptly.

Most pâtés improve if they are allowed to mature for 1–2 days, but they should be eaten within a week. Pâté made from poultry livers are the exception; they should be made and eaten within 2 days. Always use perfectly fresh ingredients for making pâtés.

MRS BEETON'S TIP

Depending on the size of the container, a house brick can be ideal for weighting pâté. Brush the brick well, wrap it in paper and seal it in a clean polythene bag to prevent any transfer of dust to the food. Place on top of the covered pâté.

PÂTÉ MAISON

8–10 rindless back bacon rashers
100 g / 4 oz pig's liver, trimmed and coarsely chopped
100 g / 4 oz rindless boned belly of pork, coarsely chopped
225 g / 8 oz sausagemeat
225 g / 8 oz cold cooked rabbit, finely chopped
1 onion, finely chopped
25 g / 1 oz fresh white breadcrumbs
1 egg, beaten
15 ml / 1 tbsp milk
75 ml / 3 fl oz brandy
salt and pepper
3 bay leaves, to garnish

Set the oven at 180°C / 350°F / gas 4. Arrange the bay leaves on the base of a 1.25-litre / 2¼-pint rectangular ovenproof dish or terrine. Lay the bacon rashers flat on a board, one at a time, and stretch them with the back of a knife until quite thin. Set aside two or three rashers for the topping and use the rest to line the dish, overlapping them neatly.

Combine the chopped liver, pork, sausagemeat, rabbit, onion and breadcrumbs in a mixing bowl. Stir in the egg, milk and brandy, with salt and pepper to taste. Spoon the mixture into the lined dish, cover with the reserved bacon rashers and then with a lid or foil. Stand the dish in a roasting tin and add enough hot water to come to within 2.5 cm / 1 inch of the rim of the tin.

When cooked, weight the pâté and leave to cool. Chill for 18–24 hours. To serve, remove the top bacon rashers and invert the pâté on a platter.

MAKES ABOUT 1 kg / 2¼ lb

CHICKEN OR TURKEY MOUSSE

225 g / 8 oz cooked chicken or turkey breast meat
275 ml / 9 fl oz double cream
275 ml / 9 fl oz chicken stock with fat removed
15 ml / 1 tbsp gelatine
3 egg yolks, beaten
salt and pepper
20 ml / 4 tsp mayonnaise
watercress sprigs and small lettuce leaves, to garnish

Remove any skin, gristle and fat from the poultry, mince it finely and place in a bowl. In a second bowl, whip the cream lightly. Chill until required. Place a mixing bowl in the refrigerator to chill.

Put 100 ml / 3½ fl oz of the stock in a heatproof bowl, sprinkle on the gelatine and set aside for 15 minutes until spongy. Put the rest of the stock in the top of a double saucepan and stir in the beaten egg yolks, with salt and pepper.

Place the pan over simmering water and cook gently, stirring frequently, until the mixture thickens slightly. Remove from the heat and pour into the chilled bowl. Stand the bowl containing the gelatine over a saucepan of hot water and stir the gelatine until it has dissolved completely. Stir into the egg mixture, mixing well. Add the minced chicken or turkey and stir until thoroughly mixed.

Stand the bowl in a basin of cold water or crushed ice, or place in the refrigerator until the mousse mixture begins to thicken at the edges. Fold in the chilled whipped cream and the mayonnaise. Turn into a wetted 1-litre / 1¾-pint mould and chill until set. To serve, turn out on to a platter and garnish.

SERVES FOUR

GRAVAD LAX

2 pieces unskinned salmon fillet, total weight about 1 kg / 2¼ lb, scaled
200 g / 7 oz salt
90g / 3¼ oz caster sugar
50 g / 2 oz white peppercorns
90 g / 3¼ oz fresh dill, plus extra to garnish

MUSTARD SAUCE

30 ml / 2 tbsp Swedish mustard (or other mild mustard)
10 ml / 2 tsp caster sugar
15 ml / 1 tbsp chopped fresh dill
45–60 ml / 3–4 tbsp sunflower oil
lemon juice to taste
salt and pepper

Score the skin on each salmon fillet in 4 places. Mix the salt, sugar and peppercorns in a bowl. Sprinkle a third of the salt mixture on the base of a shallow dish. Place one salmon fillet, skin side down, on the mixture. Cover with a further third of the salt mixture and add half the dill. Arrange the second fillet, skin side up, on top. Cover with the remaining salt mixture and dill.

Cover with foil. Place a plate or oblong baking sheet or tin on top of the fish and weight it down. Leave in the refrigerator for 36 hours, during which time the salt mixture will become a brine solution. Turn the whole fillet 'sandwich' every day and baste with the liquor.

For the sauce, mix the mustard, sugar and dill. Add the oil very slowly, beating all the time to make a thick sauce. Stir in a little lemon juice with salt and pepper to taste.

Drain off the brine and scrape away the dill and peppercorns before serving. Serve the salmon thinly sliced, garnished with fresh dill and accompanied by the mustard sauce.

SERVES FOUR TO SIX

ANGELS ON HORSEBACK

8 large shelled oysters
8 rindless streaky bacon rashers
2–3 slices of bread
butter for spreading

Wrap each oyster in a bacon rasher. Fasten the rolls with small poultry skewers, place in a grill pan and grill for 4-6 minutes. Meanwhile toast the bread. Spread with butter and cut into small fingers. Remove the skewers and serve on the toast fingers.

MAKES EIGHT

SAUCY ANGELS

6 rindlesss streaky bacon rashers
5 ml / 1 tsp finely chopped onion
2.5 ml / ½ tsp chopped parsley
125 ml / 4 fl oz thick Béchamel Sauce (page 154)
2.5 ml / ½ tsp lemon juice
paprika
salt
800 g / 1¾ lb canned or bottled mussels, drained
12 small rounds fried bread

Set the oven at 180°C / 350°F / gas 4. Using a rolling pin, stretch and flatten each rasher of bacon and cut them in half. Stir the onion and parsley into the white sauce, add the lemon juice and season with paprika and a little salt. Stir in the mussels.

Spoon 2 or 3 mussels with sauce on to each piece of bacon. Roll up carefully, securing each bacon roll with a small skewer. Place on a baking sheet and bake for 7–8 minutes. Serve hot on fried bread.

MAKES TWELVE

BURLINGTON CROÛTES

100 g / 4 oz cooked chicken or turkey, finely chopped
30 ml / 2 tbsp mayonnaise
2 tomatoes, each cut into 6 thin slices
salt and pepper
12 rounds of fried bread or crackers
butter (optional)
12 stuffed olives

Mix the chicken with the mayonnaise in a bowl. Sprinkle the tomato slices with salt and pepper. If using fried bread, drain thoroughly on absorbent kitchen paper. Butter the crackers if using. Place a slice of tomato on each bread round or cracker. Pile the chicken mixture on top. Top each croûte with a stuffed olive.

MAKES TWELVE

MRS BEETON'S PASTRY RAMAKINS

These cheese savouries can be made with the odd pieces of cheese left from a cheeseboard. Mix a little strong cheese with any mild-flavoured leftovers.

oil for greasing
225 g / 8 oz Puff Pastry (page 74)
175 g / 6 oz Stilton or Cheshire cheese, or a mixture of Parmesan and mild cheese, grated or finely crumbled
1 egg yolk

Grease a baking sheet. Set the oven at 220°C / 425°F / gas 7. Roll out the pastry into an oblong measuring about 20 x 10 cm / 8 x 4 inches. Sprinkle half the cheese over the middle of the pastry. Fold the bottom third over the cheese, then fold the top third down. Give the pastry a quarter turn clockwise, the roll it out into an oblong about the same size as the original shape.

Sprinkle the remaining cheese over the pastry and repeat the folding and rolling. Finally, roll out the pastry to about 2.5 mm / ⅛ inch thick, or slightly thicker. Use fancy cutters to stamp out shapes – fluted circles, diamonds, triangles or crescents – and place them on the baking sheet.

Stir 5 ml / 1 tsp water into the egg yolk and brush it over the pastries. Bake for 10–15 minutes, until puffed and browned. Serve fresh from the oven.

MAKES ABOUT 24

MRS BEETON'S CHEESE STRAWS

50 g / 2 oz butter
50 g / 2 oz plain flour
50 g / 2 oz soft white breadcrumbs
50 g / 2 oz Cheshire or Lancashire cheese, grated
large pinch of cayenne
salt
flour for rolling out

Rub the butter into the flour and add the breadcrumbs. Stir in the cheese along with the seasonings. Work thoroughly by hand, making a smooth dough. Cover and chill for 30 minutes.

Set the oven at 180°C / 350°F / gas 4. Roll out the dough 5 mm / 1¼ inch thick on a lightly floured surface. Cut into thin strips about 3 mm x 5 cm / ⅛ x 2 inches. Place on a greased baking sheet and bake for 7–10 minutes. Let cool on the baking sheet and serve cold.

MAKES FORTY-EIGHT TO SIXTY

HOT PEPPER CHEESES

When freshly cooked, these savouries are inclined to crumble and break easily. For this reason it is best to allow them to cool completely, then reheat gently until just warm.

butter for greasing
200 g / 7 oz plain flour
200 g / 7 oz butter
200 g / 7 oz Lancashire cheese, grated
few drops of hot pepper sauce
1.25 ml / ¼ tsp salt
flour for rolling out

Grease four baking sheets. Sift the flour into a mixing bowl and rub in the butter until the mixture resembles fine breadcrumbs. Add the cheese, hot pepper sauce and salt. Work the mixture thoroughly by hand to make a smooth dough. Use a few drops of water if necessary, but the dough will be shorter and richer without it. Chill for 30 minutes.

Meanwhile, preheat the oven to 180°C / 350°F / gas 4. Roll out the dough on a floured surface to a thickness of 5 mm / ¼ inch. Cut into rounds or shapes.

With a palette knife, transfer the shapes to the prepared baking sheets and bake for 10–12 minutes or until lightly browned and crisp. Cool on the baking sheets.

MAKES 40–50

CUTTING THE DOUGH

When cutting out the cheese dough it's best to stick to regular shapes such as rounds, crescents, squares or stars. The mixture is less likely to break if there are no thin projections.

CHEESE BUTTERFLIES

butter for greasing
100g / 4 oz plain flour
pinch of mustard powder
pinch of salt
pinch of cayenne pepper
75 g / 3 oz butter
75 g / 3 oz grated Parmesan cheese
1 egg yolk
flour for rolling out

TOPPING
100g / 4 oz cream cheese
few drops anchovy essence
few drops of red food colouring

Grease two baking sheets. Set the oven at 200°C / 400°F / gas 6. Sift the flour, mustard, salt and cayenne into a bowl. In a mixing bowl, cream the butter until soft and white, then add the flour mixture with the Parmesan. Stir in the egg yolk and enough cold water to form a stiff dough.

Roll out on a lightly floured surface to a thickness of about 3 mm / ⅛ inch and cut into rounds about 6 cm / 2¼ inches in diameter. Cut half the rounds across the centre to make 'wings'.

With a palette knife, lift both the whole rounds and the 'wings' on to the prepared baking sheets and bake for 10 minutes. Cool on the baking sheets.

Meanwhile, make the topping. Put the cream cheese in a bowl and cream until soft with a fork, adding the anchovy essence for flavour and just enough of the red food colouring to tint the mixture a pale pink. Transfer the topping to a piping bag fitted with a shell nozzle.

When the biscuits are quite cold, pipe a line of cheese across the centre of each full round and press the straight edges of two half-rounds into the cheese to make them stand up like wings.

MAKES 12-18

SPICY NUTS

30 ml / 2 tbsp salted butter
15 ml / 1 tbsp Worcestershire sauce
1.25 ml / ¼ tsp cumin
1 garlic clove, crushed with 15 ml / 1 tsp salt
1.25 ml / ¼ tsp cayenne pepper
350 g / 12 oz unsalted nuts of your choice
salt to taste

Preheat oven to 160°C / 325°F / gas 3. Melt the butter in a frying pan, over a gentle heat. Add all the ingredients except the nuts and the salt and stir for 2–3 minutes.

Add the nuts and stir until evenly coated. Spread on a baking sheet and bake for 15 to 20 minutes, shaking occasionally.

Sprinkle with salt to taste and serve immediately. Alternatively, allow to cool, store in an airtight container and serve gently reheated in a warm oven or over a moderate heat in a lightly-oiled frying pan.

ROASTING CHESTNUTS

Chestnuts, available from October to January, are the perfect fireside snack to serve with drinks. To cook them, prick the skins with a sharp knife to prevent them from bursting, spread them on a baking tray and roast them at 220ºC / 425ºF / gas 7 for 10 minutes. For a more traditional way of roasting them, put the chestnuts on a trivet or shovel over a glowing fire. Peel the nuts and serve them hot, dipped in salt.

Poultry & Game

A golden turkey is the traditional centrepiece of the Christmas table but there are many delicious alternatives in duck, goose or extravagant game dishes. This chapter includes advice on preparing and serving poultry, as well as ideas for using up any leftovers.

PREPARING POULTRY FOR COOKING

Ensure that the bird is free from any small feathers or hairs. If necessary, singe the bird to remove hairs: use long matches or a taper and allow the flame to burn for a few seconds until it has stopped smoking. Trim away any lumps of fat from the body cavity. Rinse the bird inside and out under cold water and dry it well on absorbent kitchen paper.

HYGIENE NOTE

Always thoroughly wash surfaces, the sink and all utensils that come in contact with raw poultry immediately after use. Scrub cutting boards after use. Wash your hands well, paying attention to nails, and dry them thoroughly before preparing other food.

STUFFING POULTRY

Never stuff a bird more than an hour before cooking it. The stuffing may be prepared in advance and kept separately in a covered container in the refrigerator. Stuffing may be placed in the body cavity of the bird or under the skin covering the breast.

To insert stuffing under the skin, first loosen the skin by inserting the point of a knife between it and the flesh at the neck end of the bird. Once the skin is loosened, wash and dry your hands, then work your fingers up between the flesh and skin to form a pocket over the breast meat. Take care not to split the skin. Thoroughly clean your hands.

Use a spoon to insert the stuffing into the prepared pocket, easing it in place by moulding it with the skin on the outside. When the stuffing is in place, use a skewer to secure the end of the skin to the bird.

PREPARATION TECHNIQUES

The majority of poultry nowadays is sold ready for cooking. If any special preparation is required, a good butcher will almost certainly do this willingly, given sufficient notice, but it is useful to know the basics of trussing and jointing poultry.

JOINTING

You'll need a large, heavy cook's knife. A pair of poultry shears or strong kitchen scissors are also useful and a meat mallet or rolling pin may be necessary to tap the blade of the knife through areas of bone. There are many ways of jointing poultry; this is one method:

- Pull the leg away from the body, cut through the skin, then break the joint away above the thigh.
- Cut through the meat between the thigh and drumstick and separate the two portions.
- Cut through the breast down to the wing joint, taking a portion of breast meat and removing it with the whole wing joint.
- Turn the bird over, so that the breast is down. Cut the carcass in half through the middle, tapping the knife with a meat mallet. Cut away the ends of the breast bone and any small bits of bone. Turn the breast over and split in half.

SPATCHCOCK

- Turn the bird breast down. Cut off the parson's nose. Using a heavy cook's knife, cut through the skin, flesh and bone down the length of the bird to open the carcass. Do not cut right through to the breast. Open the carcass out and turn it over so that the breast is uppermost.
- Place the palm of your hand on the top of the breast and flatten the bird by pressing down firmly with your other hand. The spatchcocked bird may be kept flat by threading two metal skewers through it.

BONING POULTRY

Have ready a sharp, pointed cook's knife. A pair of kitchen scissors is also useful for snipping flesh and sinew free from joint ends.

- Lay the bird breast down. Cut through the skin and flesh right in to the bone along the length of the back. Beginning at one end of the slit, slide the point of the knife under the flesh and skin. Keeping the knife close to the bone, cut the meat off the bone. Work all the meat off the bone on one side of the carcass, going down the rib cage as far as the breast. Leave the breast meat attached to the soft bone.
- Cut off the wing ends, leaving only the first part of the joint in place. To free the flesh from the wing joint, carefully scrape the meat off the first part, using scissors or the point of the knife to cut sinews.

- Pull the bones and meat apart as though removing an arm from a sleeve. Again use the point of a knife or scissors to cut sinew and skin attached at the bone end. This leaves the flesh and skin turned inside-out and the bones free but attached to the carcass. Turn the flesh and skin back out the right way. Repeat the process with the leg.
- Turn the bird around and repeat the process on the second side, again leaving the breast meat attached to the soft bone.
- When all the meat is removed from the second side, and the joints have been boned, the carcass will remain attached along the breast bone. Taking care not to cut the skin, lift the carcass away from the meat and cut along the breast bone, taking the finest sliver of soft bone to avoid damaging the skin.
- Spread out the boned bird. It is now ready for stuffing. To reshape it, simply fold the sides over the stuffing and sew them with a trussing needle and cooking thread. Turn the bird over with the seam down and plump it up into a neat shape, tucking the boned joint meat under.

ROASTING POULTRY

The cooking time should be calculated according to the weight of the prepared bird, with stuffing, if used. Place the bird in a roasting tin; using a rack or trivet if liked. A goose should always be cooked on a rack over a deep tin so that the large amount of fat drips away. Brush the bird with a little melted butter or oil if required and sprinkle with seasoning (see individual recipes for more detailed information). A large chicken or turkey may have its breast covered with streaky bacon to prevent the meat from drying out. Turkey should be covered with foil for part of the cooking time to prevent overbrowning.

Chicken does not usually require turning during cooking. Duck may be turned once or twice but this is not essential. Goose and turkey should be turned several times, depending on size, to promote moist, even cooking. All poultry should be basted during cooking. The following times are a general guide but may vary according to the exact ingredients used and the oven temperature, as when a bird is marinated and coated with seasonings that affect the browning.

- **Chicken and Guineafowl** Allow 20 minutes per 450 g / 1 lb plus 20 minutes at 180°C / 350°F / gas 4.
- **Duck** Prick the duck all over with a fork or skewer to release the fat. Roast on a rack, allowing 15–20 minutes per 450 g / 1 lb at 190–200°C / 375–400°F / gas 5–6.
- **Goose** Allow 20–25 minutes per 450 g / 1 lb at 180°C / 350°F / gas 4.

- **Turkey** This requires long, slow cooking to ensure that the meat is thoroughly cooked. This is particularly important if the body cavity of the bird is stuffed. The following times are at 180ºC / 350ºF / gas 4. Keep the bird covered with foil until the final 30–45 minutes of cooking. These times are a guide only, based upon the bird's weight excluding stuffing, since it is not easy to weigh a stuffed turkey. Birds without stuffing will take slightly less time to cook.

Weight (before stuffing)	**Time at 180ºC / 350ºF / gas 4**
2.5 kg / 5½ lb	2½–3 hours
2.75–3.5 kg / 6–8 lb	3–3¾ hours
3.5–4.5 kg / 8–10 lb	3¾–4½ hours
4.5–5.5 kg / 10–12 lb	4½–5 hours
5.5–11.4 kg / 12–25 lb	20 minutes per 450 g / 1 lb plus 20 minutes

- **Microwave Cooking** Lean, tender poultry cooks well in the microwave, although whole chickens and ducks benefit from being partially cooked by this method, then placed in a conventional oven to crisp the skin. Follow the instructions that came with your microwave.

TESTING FOR COOKING PROGRESS

It is essential that chicken and turkey are thoroughly cooked right through. With large birds, increasing the cooking temperature will not necessarily speed up the process as lengthy cooking must be allowed to ensure the thick areas of meat and the body cavity reach a high temperature.

To test, pierce the meat at a thick point – for example on the thigh behind the drumstick. Check for any signs of blood in the juices and for any meat that appears pink or uncooked. When the bird is cooked, the juices will run clear and the meat will be firm and white right through to the bone. On a large bird test in at least two places to ensure that all the meat is well cooked.

CARVING

The same rules apply to all poultry: the breast is carved in neat slices, working at an angle to the carcass to yield several slices of a similar size from each side. The wings and legs are then removed. To make it easier to carve the breast on chickens and smaller birds, the wings and legs are usually removed and served as individual portions. This is not necessary when carving larger birds, such as turkey, as the breast meat can easily be sliced off with the joints still in place.

FREEZING AND THAWING POULTRY

Poultry for freezing should be absolutely fresh. Never allow the use-by date to expire before freezing poultry; when buying from a butcher always check that the bird is suitably fresh for freezing, or that portions have not previously been frozen.

Never re-freeze poultry once it has been thawed.

Prepare birds as for cooking and pack them in heavy-quality airtight bags, labelled with the date and weight or number of portions. Breasts, drumsticks, fillets or other portions may be individually wrapped in freezer film before being packed in bags. Cubed meat or strips of meat should be loosely packed in sealed bags. The bags should then be spread out thinly on a baking sheet until the meat is hard. When hard the meat may be shaken down in the bag and any extra air extracted – this method creates a 'free-flow' pack, permitting some of the meat to be used as required and the rest replaced in the freezer without thawing. If available, use the fast freeze facility on your freezer to process the poultry as speedily as possible. Follow the freezer manufacturer's instructions.

Always allow sufficient time for thawing poultry in the refrigerator before cooking. It is also possible to thaw poultry in the microwave oven following the appliance manufacturer's instructions. Both chicken and turkey must be cooked through before serving; if the whole bird or portions are not thoroughly thawed before cooking, thick areas of meat may not cook through. Due to its size, whole turkey is the most difficult poultry to thaw.

Always unwrap poultry and place it in a covered deep dish in the refrigerator, preferably on a low shelf, ensuring that it will not drip on any other food. Occasionally, drain off the liquid which seeps from the poultry as it thaws. Allow several hours or up to 24 hours for portions and smaller birds to thaw. Large poultry such as turkeys are usually purchased fresh; when buying frozen birds always read and follow the recommendations listed on the wrapping. The following is a guide to recommended thawing times by weight in the refrigerator: these times are not exact and they can only act as a guide. As soon as it is possible to do so, remove the giblets, and cook them to make stock. Cool the stock and freeze it until required. This is preferable to storing the stock in the refrigerator for several days while the turkey continues to thaw.

Weight of turkey	**Thawing time in refrigerator**
2.5–3.5 kg / 5½–8 lb	up to 2½ days
3.5–5.5 kg / 8–12 lb	2½–3 days
5.5–7.25 kg / 12–16 lb	3–4 days
7.25–9 kg / 16–20 lb	4–4½ days

MRS BEETON'S ROAST TURKEY

The recipe that follows is based upon a 6 kg / 13 lb bird. Timings for birds of different weights are given in the introduction to this section, which also includes information on thawing frozen birds, tips for successful cooking and advice on carving.

fat for basting
1 turkey
450 g / 1 lb Mrs Beeton's Forcemeat (page 139)
675 g / 1½ lb seasoned sausagemeat
225 g / 8 oz rindless streaky bacon rashers

Set the oven at 220°C / 425°F / gas 7. Weigh the turkey. Trim it, and wash it inside and out in cold water. Pat dry with absorbent kitchen paper. Immediately before cooking, stuff the neck of the bird with forcemeat. Put the sausagemeat inside the body cavity. Cover the breast of the bird with the bacon rashers.

Place the prepared turkey in a roasting tin. Cover with foil and roast for 15 minutes. Lower the oven temperature to 180°C / 350°F / gas 4 and roast for 20 minutes per 450 g / 1lb (unstuffed weight) plus 20 minutes, or until cooked through. Remove the foil for the last hour of cooking and the bacon strips for the final 20 minutes to allow the breast to brown.

Serve on a heated platter, with roasted or grilled chipolata sausages, Bacon Rolls (see page 47) and Bread Sauce (see page 144).

SERVES FOURTEEN TO SIXTEEN

MRS BEETON'S TIP

Lemons, cut in half and with all flesh and pulp removed, make ideal containers for individual portions of cranberry sauce. Arrange them around the turkey.

ROAST TURKEY WITH CHESTNUTS

1 x 4.5–5.5 kg / 10–12 lb turkey
salt and pepper
225 g / 8 oz rindless streaky bacon rashers

HERB FORCEMEAT
50 g / 2 oz margarine
100 g / 4 oz fresh white breadcrumbs
pinch of grated nutmeg
15 ml / 1 tbsp chopped parsley
5 ml / 1 tsp chopped fresh mixed herbs
grated rind of ½ lemon
salt and pepper
1 egg, beaten

CHESTNUT STUFFING
1 kg / 2¼ lb chestnuts
275 ml / 9¾ fl oz turkey or chicken stock
50 g / 2 oz butter
1 egg, beaten
single cream or milk (see method)

First make the chestnut stuffing. Shell and skin the chestnuts (see pages 3 and 111). Put them in a saucepan, add the stock and simmer for 20 minutes or until tender. Drain the chestnuts and chop them finely, or press through a sieve into a clean bowl. Melt the butter in a small saucepan. Remove from the heat and add to the bowl containing the chestnuts. Stir in the beaten egg, with enough cream or milk to moisten the mixture.

Make the forcemeat. Melt the margarine in a small saucepan. Add the breadcrumbs, nutmeg, herbs and lemon rind. Stir in salt and pepper to taste and sufficient beaten egg to bind the mixture.

Set the oven at 180°C / 350°F / gas 4. Trim the turkey and wash it inside and out in cold water. Pat dry with absorbent kitchen paper and season inside with salt and pepper. Immediately before cooking, fill the neck end of the bird with chestnut stuffing and the body with the forcemeat. Truss if wished, and cover the bird with the bacon.

Place the bird in a roasting tin and roast for 4½–5 hours or until cooked through, removing the bacon towards the end to allow the breast to brown. Serve with giblet gravy.

SERVES FOURTEEN TO SIXTEEN

BACON ROLLS

Cut the rinds from streaky bacon rashers, cut each rasher in half crossways and roll up. To fry, secure the outer end with a wooden toothpick inserted along each roll. To grill, thread the rolls on short skewers. Put in a dry frying pan or under a moderate grilling heat, and fry or grill for 3-5 minutes, turning frequently, until crisp.

ALLOW 2 BACON ROLLS (1 RASHER) PER PERSON.

IDEAS FOR LEFTOVER ROAST TURKEY

- **Hashed Turkey** Make stock from turkey bones and trimmings, a sliced carrot, a diced turnip, a blade of mace and a bouquet garni. Cover with water and simmer for 1 hour. Strain. Cook 1 chopped onion in a knob of butter. Add 40 g / 1½ oz plain flour and cook for 2 minutes. Pour in 600 ml / 1 pint strained stock and bring to the boil. Add 30 ml / 2 tbsp mushroom ketchup, 45 ml / 3 tbsp port or sherry and salt and pepper. Gently poach sliced cooked turkey in the sauce, adding any leftover stuffing cut in neat portions, for 15 minutes until thoroughly heated.
- **Turkey Croquettes** Mince or finely chop cooked turkey – this is ideal for dark meat and small pieces which do not slice well. For every 225 g / 8 oz turkey, allow 50 g / 2 oz diced or minced cooked ham and ½ small finely chopped onion. Cook the onion in a little butter, stir in 15 ml / 1 tbsp plain flour and 150 ml / ¼ pint turkey gravy or stock. Bring to the boil. Remove from the heat and add the turkey, ham, 1 egg yolk and plenty of seasoning. Cool, then chill. Shape the mixture into croquettes. Coat in flour, egg and breadcrumbs, then deep or shallow fry until golden. Originally, the mixture was shaped into small mounds by pressing it into a small, greased wine glass before coating.

See also Turkey Soup (page 13), Chicken and Turkey Mousse (page 31), Burlington Croûtes (page 34), Devilled Turkey (page 49), Turkey and Chipolata Hotpot (page 50), Turkey Loaf (page 51), Poultry with Peas (page 60), Poultry à la Béchamel (page 62) and Poultry Fritters (page 63).

DEVILLED TURKEY

550 g / 1¼ lb cold roast turkey

DEVILLING BUTTER
50 g / 2 oz butter
large pinch cayenne
large pinch of ground black pepper
5 ml / 1 tsp curry paste
pinch of ground ginger

BARBECUE SAUCE
30 ml / 2 tbsp oil
1 onion, finely chopped
2 garlic cloves, crushed
1 x 397 g / 14 oz can chopped tomatoes
45 ml / 3 tbsp red wine vinegar
30 ml / 2 tbsp soft dark brown sugar
30 ml / 2 tbsp tomato ketchup
10 ml / 2 tsp soy sauce
10 ml / 2 tsp Worcestershire sauce
salt and pepper

Mix together all the ingredients for the devilling butter.

Divide the turkey into convenient portions for serving, remove the skin and score the flesh deeply. Spread lightly with the prepared butter and leave for 1 hour (or longer if a highly seasoned dish is required).

Now make the barbecue sauce. Heat the oil in a saucepan. Add the onion and garlic and fry over gentle heat for 4–6 minutes, until the onion is soft but not coloured. Stir in the remaining ingredients and bring to the boil. Lower the heat and simmer for 30–45 minutes, until the sauce is thick and well-flavoured.

Grill the turkey for about 8 minutes, turning once, until crisp and brown. Serve with the barbecue sauce.

SERVES SIX

TURKEY AND CHIPOLATA HOTPOT

This is an excellent way of using up leftovers from a roast turkey. Cooked chicken may be used instead of turkey and the chipolatas will extend a small amount of meat to serve four.

15 ml / 1 tbsp oil
225 g / 8 oz cocktail or chipolata sausages
1 onion, halved and sliced
2 carrots, diced
2 parsnips, diced
1 bay leaf
5 ml / 1 tsp dried sage
45 ml / 3 tbsp plain flour
300 ml / ½ pint medium cider
300 ml / ½ pint turkey or chicken stock
350 g / 12 oz cooked turkey, diced
salt and pepper
100 g / 4 oz frozen peas

Heat the oil in a large flameproof casserole until it runs easily over the base. Add the cocktail sausages or chipolatas and turn them in the oil. Sprinkle the onion into the pan and cook, turning occasionally, until the sausages are evenly and lightly browned but not necessarily cooked through.

Add the carrots, parsnips, bay leaf and sage to the casserole. Cover and cook gently for 15 minutes. Stir in the flour, then gradually stir in the cider and stock and bring to the boil. Add the turkey, with salt and pepper to taste, then cover and simmer for 10 minutes, or until the vegetables are tender.

Stir in the peas, replace the cover and simmer for a further 10– 15 minutes, until the vegetables are all tender. Taste and adjust the seasoning before serving. If using chipolatas, cut them into bite-sized chunks.

SERVES FOUR

TURKEY LOAF

oil for greasing
50 g / 2 oz long-grain rice
225 g / 8 oz cooked turkey meat
4 rindless streaky bacon rashers
salt and pepper
1 onion, finely chopped
about 50 ml / 2 fl oz turkey or chicken stock
grated rind and juice of ½ lemon
50 g / 2 oz fresh white breadcrumbs
2.5 ml / ½ tsp chopped fresh thyme
5 ml / 1 tsp chopped parsley
15 ml / 1 tbsp milk

Grease a 450-g / 1-lb loaf tin. Set the oven at 190°C / 375°F / gas 5. Cook the rice in a saucepan of boiling salted water for 20 minutes, then drain and set aside.

Mince the turkey meat with the bacon. Put the mixture in a bowl and add plenty of salt and pepper. Stir in the onion, stock, lemon rind and rice.

In a separate bowl, mix the breadcrumbs, thyme, parsley and lemon juice. Add a little salt and pepper and mix in the milk to bind this stuffing.

Put half the turkey mixture in the prepared tin, spread with the stuffing, then cover with the remaining turkey mixture. Bake for about 35 minutes, until firm and browned on top. Turn out and serve hot or cold.

SERVES SIX TO EIGHT

ROAST GOOSE WITH APPLES AND ONIONS

1 goose with giblets
salt and pepper
1 orange
1 lemon
13 small onions
7 bay leaves
1 large fresh thyme sprig
30 ml / 2 tbsp dried sage
1 cinnamon stick
4 cloves
50 g / 2 oz butter
12 Cox's Orange Pippin apples
5 ml / 1 tsp lemon juice
45 ml / 3 tbsp port
45 ml / 3 tbsp crab apple or redcurrant jelly
25 g / 1 oz plain flour

Remove the giblets from the goose and put them in a saucepan. Add 1.5 litres / 2¾ pints water and bring to the boil. Lower the heat and simmer until the liquid is reduced by half. Strain and set aside.

Set the oven at 230°C / 450°F / gas 8. Weigh the goose and calculate the cooking time at 20 minutes per 450 g / 1 lb. Trim away excess fat and rinse the bird, then rub it all over with plenty of salt and pepper. Pare the rind from the fruit and place it in the body cavity with 1 onion, 2 bay leaves and the thyme sprig. Rub the sage over the outside of the bird and tuck a bay leaf behind each of the wing and leg joints.

Place the goose on a rack in a roasting tin. Place it in the oven and immediately reduce the heat to 180°C / 350°F / gas 4. Cook for the calculated time, draining away fat from the roasting tin occasionally.

Peel the remaining onions but leave them whole. Place them in a saucepan and pour in boiling water to cover. Add a little salt. Simmer for 15 minutes, then drain well. Squeeze the juice from the orange and lemon, and mix together in a small saucepan. Add the cinnamon, cloves and remaining bay leaf, then heat gently until simmering. Cover and cook for 15 minutes. Remove from the heat and stir in the butter.

Peel and core the apples. As each apple is prepared, place it in a bowl of iced water to which the lemon juice has been added. This will prevent discoloration. Drain the apples, put them in an ovenproof dish and spoon the fruit juice and spice mixture over them to coat them completely. Add the onions, then toss them with the apples so all are coated in juices.

Place the dish of apples and onions in the oven 1 hour before the goose is cooked. Turn them occasionally during cooking so that they are evenly browned and tender. About 10 minutes before the goose is cooked, heat the port and jelly gently in a saucepan or in a bowl in the microwave until the jelly has melted. Spoon this over the apple and onion mixture for the final 5 minutes.

When the goose is cooked, transfer it to a heated serving platter and keep hot. Drain off the fat from the tin. Stir the flour into the cooking juices and cook over low heat for 5 minutes, scraping in all the sediment from the base of the pan. Pour in the reserved giblet stock and bring to the boil, stirring all the time. Taste for seasoning and pour or strain into a sauceboat.

Serve the goose surrounded by the glazed apples and onions, with their juices.

SERVES SIX
(WITH MEAT TO SPARE, DEPENDING ON THE SIZE OF THE GOOSE)

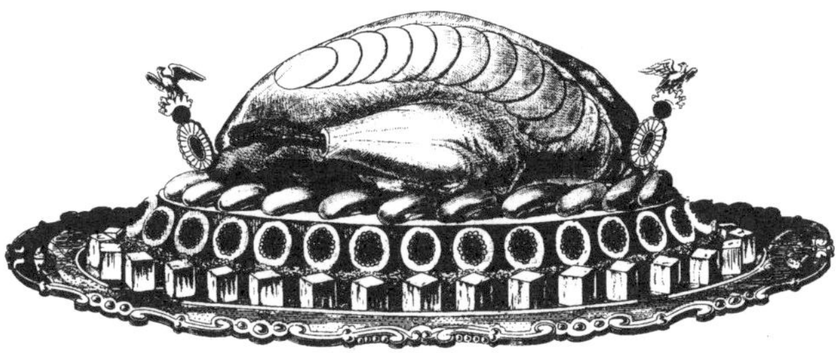

ROAST GOOSE WITH FRUIT STUFFING AND RED CABBAGE

1 goose with giblets
½ lemon
salt and pepper
350 g / 12 oz prunes, soaked overnight in water to cover
450 g / 1 lb cooking apples
15 ml / 1 tbsp redcurrant jelly

RED CABBAGE
50 g / 2 oz butter
1. 5 kg / 3¼ lb red cabbage, finely shredded
50 g / 2 oz demerara sugar
75 ml / 5 tbsp malt or cider vinegar
salt and pepper

Remove the giblets from the goose and put them in a saucepan. Add 1.5 litres / 2¾ pints water and bring to the boil. Lower the heat and simmer until the liquid is reduced by half. Strain and set aside.

Set the oven at 230°C / 450°F / gas 8. Weigh the goose and calculate the cooking time at 20 minutes per 450 g / 1 lb. Remove the excess fat usually found around the vent. Rinse the inside of the bird, then rub the skin with lemon. Season with salt and pepper.

Drain the prunes, remove the stones and roughly chop the flesh. Put it in a bowl. Peel, core and chop the apples. Add them to the prunes, with salt and pepper to taste. Use the mixture to stuff the body of the bird. Put the goose on a rack in a roasting tin. Place in the oven, immediately lower the temperature to 180°C / 350°F / gas 4 and cook for the calculated time. Drain away fat from the roasting tin occasionally during cooking.

Meanwhile, melt the butter in a large flameproof casserole, add the red cabbage and sugar and stir well. Pour in 75 ml / 5 tbsp water and the vinegar, adding salt and pepper to taste. Cover and cook in the oven for about 2 hours, stirring occasionally.

When the goose is cooked, transfer it to a heated serving platter and keep hot. Drain off the excess fat from the roasting tin, retaining the juices. Stir in the reserved giblet stock and cook over fairly high heat until reduced to a thin gravy. Stir in the redcurrant jelly until melted. Serve the gravy and red cabbage separately.

SERVES SIX TO EIGHT

ROAST CHICKEN WITH HONEY AND ALMONDS

1 x 1.5–1.8 kg / 3½–4 lb oven-ready roasting chicken
½ lemon
salt and pepper
45 ml / 3 tbsp honey
50 g / 2 oz flaked almonds
pinch of powdered saffron
30 ml / 2 tbsp oil
watercress sprigs, to garnish (optional)

Set the oven at 180°C / 350°F / gas 4. Rub the chicken all over with the cut lemon, then sprinkle with salt and pepper. Line a roasting tin with a piece of foil large enough to enclose the bird completely.

Put the bird into the foil-lined tin, then brush it all over with the honey. Sprinkle with the nuts and saffron, then trickle the oil very gently over the top. Bring up the foil carefully, tenting it over the bird so that it is completely covered. Make sure that the foil does not touch the skin. Seal the package by folding the edges of the foil over.

Roast for 1½–2 hours or until the chicken is cooked through. Open the foil for the last 10 minutes to allow the breast of the bird to brown. Transfer the chicken to a heated serving dish and garnish it with watercress if liked.

SERVES FOUR TO SIX

BRAISED CHESTNUT CHICKEN

1 x 1.4–1.6 kg / 3–3½ lb chicken
flour for coating
salt and pepper
45 ml / 3 tbsp oil
1 onion, sliced
3 rindless streaky bacon rashers, cut into strips
300 ml / ½ pint chicken stock
30 ml / 2 tbsp plain flour
25 g / 1 oz butter
450 g / 1 lb chipolata sausages, fried or grilled, to garnish

CHESTNUT AND HAM STUFFING
450 g / 1 lb chestnuts
250–300 ml / 9–10 fl oz chicken stock
50 g / 2 oz cooked ham, finely chopped
100 g / 4 oz fresh white breadcrumbs
grated rind of 1 lemon
2–3 parsley sprigs, chopped
25 g / 1 oz butter, melted
1 egg, beaten

Start by making the stuffing. Remove the shells and skins of the chestnuts (see pages 3 and 111). Place the cleaned nuts in a saucepan, just cover with stock and bring to the boil. Cover, lower the heat until the liquid is only just boiling, and cook for about 20 minutes or until the nuts are tender. Drain and mash them, or press them through a fine sieve into a bowl.

Stir in the ham, breadcrumbs, lemon rind and parsley, with salt and pepper to taste. Add the melted butter with enough of the beaten egg to bind. Stuff the chicken with this mixture and truss it.

Spread out the flour in a large shallow bowl. Season with salt and pepper. Add the chicken, turning and rolling it in the mixture until well coated. Heat the oil in a large, heavy-bottomed flameproof casserole or saucepan with a lid.

Fry the bird on all sides until lightly browned, then remove it. Add the onion and bacon to the oil remaining in the pan and fry for 4–5 minutes over gentle heat until the onion is slightly softened but not coloured. Replace the chicken in the pan. Pour in the stock, cover the pan and bring just to the boil. Lower the heat and simmer for 1½ hours or until the chicken is cooked through, adding more chicken stock or water as necessary.

Carefully remove the chicken from the pan. Use a large spoon to skim the fat from the cooking liquid, then process the remaining juices in a blender or food processor, or push them through a sieve into a clean saucepan. In a small bowl, blend the flour with the butter. Bring the sieved liquid to the boil, then reduce the heat so it simmers steadily. Gradually add small pieces of the flour and butter mixture to the cooking juices remaining in the pan, whisking thoroughly after each addition. Whisk until the sauce is thickened. Simmer for 3 minutes, whisking occasionally, add salt and pepper to taste and pour into a sauceboat.

Serve the chicken surrounded by fried or grilled chipolatas. Offer the sauce separately.

SERVES FOUR TO SIX

ENGLISH ROAST DUCK

fat for basting
Sage and Onion Stuffing (page 136)
1 x 1.8 kg / 4 lb oven-ready duck
salt and pepper
30 ml / 2 tbsp plain flour
300 ml / ½ pint duck stock or Chicken Stock (page 18)
(see Mrs Beeton's Tip)

Set the oven at 190°C / 375°F / gas 5. Spoon the stuffing into the duck and truss it. Weigh the duck and calculate the cooking time at 20 minutes per 450 g / 1 lb. Sprinkle the breast with salt. Put the duck on a wire rack in a roasting tin and prick the skin all over with a fork or skewer to release the fat. Roast for the required time, basting the duck occasionally with the pan juices and pouring away the excess fat as necessary. Test by piercing the thickest part of the thigh with the point of a sharp knife. The juices should run clear.

Transfer the duck to a heated platter, remove the trussing string and keep hot. Pour off most of the fat from the roasting tin, sprinkle in the flour and cook, stirring, for 2 minutes. Blend in the stock. Bring to the boil, then lower the heat and simmer, stirring, for 3–4 minutes. Add salt and pepper to taste. Serve in a gravyboat, with the duck.

SERVES FOUR

MRS BEETON'S TIP

If you have the duck giblets, use them as the basis of your stock. Put them in a saucepan with 1 sliced onion and 1 sliced carrot. Add 600 ml / 1 pint water. Simmer, covered, for 1 hour, then strain.

DUCK AND RED CABBAGE

The trimmings from two roast ducks should yield enough meat for this flavoursome dish.

50 g / 2 oz butter
450 g / 1 lb red cabbage, shredded
salt and pepper
well-flavoured stock (see method)
about 400 g / 14 oz cold roast duck, shredded
15 ml / 1 tbsp red wine vinegar
15 ml / 1 tbsp demerara sugar

Melt the butter in a heavy-bottomed saucepan and add the red cabbage. Stir lightly to coat the cabbage in butter, then add salt and pepper. Cover the pan tightly and simmer for 1 hour. Shake the pan from time to time to prevent the cabbage from sticking to the base, and add just enough stock to prevent it from burning.

In another pan, combine the duck with enough stock to moisten. Place over gentle heat until the duck is heated through. Add the vinegar and sugar to the cabbage, mix well, then turn on to a heated dish. Drain the duck and arrange it on the top. Serve with a mixture of brown rice and wild rice, if liked.

SERVES FOUR TO SIX

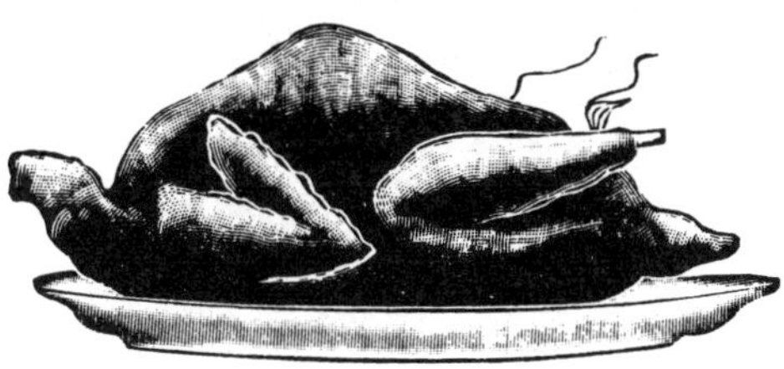

POULTRY WITH PEAS

350 g / 12 oz cooked chicken, turkey, duck or goose, cut in neat pieces
salt and pepper
2.5 ml / ½ tsp ground mace
30 ml / 2 tbsp plain flour
50 g / 2 oz butter or 25 g / 1 oz butter and 15 ml / 1 tbsp oil
300 ml / ½ pint poultry or giblet stock
450 g / 1 lb shelled peas
5 ml / 1 tsp sugar

Place the poultry in a small bowl. Add plenty of salt and pepper, the mace and flour and mix well. Melt the butter, or heat the butter and oil, in a heavy-bottomed saucepan. Add the poultry, reserving any flour in the bowl, and brown the pieces lightly.

Stir in any remaining flour, then gradually pour in the stock and bring to the boil, stirring. Add the peas, reduce the heat so that the sauce simmers and cover the pan. Cook for 20 minutes, until the peas are tender. Stir in the sugar and check the seasoning before serving.

SERVES FOUR

POULTRY PILAU

350 g / 12 oz basmati rice
50 g / 2 oz butter
4 boneless poultry breast fillets, skinned
6 cardamoms
4 cloves
15 ml / 1 tbsp coriander seeds, crushed
15 ml / 1 tbsp allspice berries, crushed
1 cinnamon stick
1 blade of mace
salt and pepper
1.1 litres / 2 pints chicken stock
15 ml / 1 tbsp oil
4 onions, thinly sliced
8 thin rindless bacon rashers
2 eggs, hard-boiled and quartered

Wash the basmati rice in several changes of water, then drain it in a sieve. Melt half the butter in a flameproof casserole or heavy-bottomed saucepan. Add the poultry breasts and brown them well all over. Sprinkle all the spices, salt and pepper around the poultry and cook for 2 minutes, then add the rice. Pour in the stock and bring to the boil. Reduce the heat, cover the pan tightly and cook the pilau gently for about 30 minutes, until the chicken is cooked and the stock is absorbed. Leave to stand, covered, off the heat for 5 minutes before removing the lid.

Meanwhile, melt the remaining butter with the oil in a large frying pan. Add the onions and a little salt and pepper. Then cook, turning the slices occasionally, until golden brown. Roll the bacon rashers and thread them onto metal skewers. Cook under a hot grill until crisp and golden, then drain on absorbent kitchen paper.

Mound the cooked pilau on a heated serving dish. Top with the browned onions. Garnish with the bacon rolls and eggs.

SERVES FOUR

POULTRY À LA BÉCHAMEL

If you have only a small amount of leftover roast poultry, add some sliced mushrooms or diced cooked ham to the sauce as well.

leftovers from a roast chicken or turkey, cut into neat pieces
600 ml / 1 pint Béchamel Sauce (page 154)
salt and pepper
2 eggs, separated
25 g / 1 oz butter, melted
60 ml / 4 tbsp dried white breadcrumbs
30 ml / 2 tbsp grated Parmesan cheese

Set the oven at 200°C / 400°F / gas 6. Stir the poultry into the sauce and add salt and pepper to taste. Stir in the egg yolks and the butter, then turn the mixture into an ovenproof dish – a pie dish is ideal.

In a perfectly clean bowl, whisk the egg whites until stiff. Gently fold in the breadcrumbs and Parmesan cheese – don't be too fussy about thoroughly combining the ingredients, it's more important to retain air in the egg white.

Turn the egg white mixture out on top of the poultry in sauce and spread it out evenly. Bake for 20 minutes, until the topping is golden brown and the chicken mixture is thoroughly heated. Serve at once.

SERVES FOUR

POULTRY FRITTERS

These fritters may be garnished with parsley and Bacon Rolls (page 47). Originally, gravy or a sauce may have been offered with them; however, they are best served with lemon wedges for their juice and a crisp salad to complement the rich batter.

225–350 g / 8–12 oz cooked chicken, turkey, duck or goose, cut in neat pieces
salt
cayenne pepper
5 ml / 1 tsp wine vinegar
2–3 shallots or ½ onion, finely chopped
5 ml / 1 tsp grated lemon rind
ground mace or grated nutmeg
oil for deep frying

BATTER
100 g / 4 oz plain flour
25 g / 1 oz butter, melted
1 egg white

Place the poultry in a bowl. Add plenty of salt, a pinch of cayenne, the vinegar, shallots or onion, lemon rind and a pinch of mace or a little grated nutmeg. Mix well, then leave to marinate for 1 hour.

Heat the oil for deep frying to 190°C / 375°F or until a cube of bread browns in 30 seconds. To make the batter, sift the flour into a bowl. Stir in 200 ml / 7 fl oz hand-hot water and the butter, then beat well until smooth. In a separate bowl, whisk the egg white until stiff. Fold the white into the batter.

Coat pieces of the marinated poultry in the batter, then deep fry them until crisp and golden. Very small offcuts may be cooked together to make bite-sized fritters. Drain on absorbent kitchen paper. Serve piping hot.

SERVES FOUR

ROAST GUINEAFOWL

50 g / 2 oz butter
salt and pepper
1 guineafowl
2 rindless fat bacon rashers
flour for dredging

GARNISH
watercress sprigs
30 ml / 2 tbsp French dressing

Set the oven at 180°C / 350°F / gas 4. Mix the butter in a small bowl with plenty of salt and pepper. Put most of the seasoned butter inside the body of the bird. Spread the rest on the thighs. Lay the bacon rashers over the breast.

Put the bird in a roasting tin and roast for 1–1½ hours or until cooked through, basting frequently. When the bird is almost cooked, remove the bacon rashers, dredge the breast with flour, baste with the juices and finish cooking.

Wash and dry the watercress. Put it in a bowl, add about 30 ml / 2 tbsp French dressing and toss lightly. Remove any trussing strings from the bird, place it on a serving dish and garnish.

SERVES TWO TO THREE

GUINEAFOWL WITH GRAPES

The guineafowl may be stuffed with Wild Rice Stuffing (page 136). Select the longer cooking time. Guineafowl is a farmed bird which is hung to give a mild, game-like flavour.

1 guineafowl with giblets
1 bouquet garni
salt and pepper
50 g / 2 oz butter
1 parsley sprig
6 rindless streaky bacon rashers
30 ml / 2 tbsp plain flour
125 ml / 4 fl oz dry white wine
225 g / 8 oz seedless white grapes
lemon juice (see method)
lemon cups filled with seedless red grapes or redcurrant jelly, to garnish

Put the guineafowl giblets in a saucepan. Add 250 ml / 9 fl oz water, the bouquet garni, salt and pepper. Bring to the boil, lower the heat and simmer for 40 minutes to make a good stock. Strain the stock and reserve 150 ml / ¼ pint.

Set the oven at 180°C / 350°F / gas 4. Put a knob of butter and the parsley inside the bird; spread the rest of the butter over the breast. Cover with the bacon. Put the bird in a roasting tin and roast for 1–1½ hours, basting frequently. Remove the bacon rashers for the last 15 minutes to allow the breast to brown.

Remove the guineafowl from the roasting tin. Cut it into neat serving portions, arrange on a heated serving dish and keep hot. Drain the fat from the tin, leaving just sufficient to absorb the flour. Sprinkle the flour into the tin and brown lightly. Stir in the wine and reserved stock. Bring the gravy to the boil, stirring constantly, then add the grapes. Add a little lemon juice to bring out the flavour and heat through, stirring constantly. Taste the sauce and add more salt and pepper if required. Pour the sauce over the guineafowl. Garnish with lemon cups (half-lemons with flesh scooped out) filled with small red seedless grapes or redcurrant jelly and serve.

SERVES THREE TO FOUR

NORMANDY PARTRIDGES

Serve simple, but interesting, vegetables to accompany this old-fashioned French dish. Tiny scrubbed potatoes, baked in their jackets, lightly steamed French beans and carrots cut into thin julienne strips are all ideal.

100 g / 4 oz unsalted butter
2 young partridges
salt and pepper
2 rindless streaky bacon rashers
675 g / 1½ lb eating apples
125 ml / 4 fl oz double cream
30 ml / 2 tbsp Calvados or brandy
chopped parsley to garnish

Set the oven at 180°C / 350°F / gas 4. Heat half the butter in a flameproof casserole, add the partridges and brown them on all sides. Sprinkle with salt and pepper. Place a bacon rasher on each bird's breast. Peel, core and cut the apples into wedges. Melt the remaining butter in a frying pan, add the apples and cover the pan. Cook gently for 5 minutes, then add to the casserole. Cook in the oven for 20–30 minutes. Transfer the partridges and apples to a hot serving dish.

Mix the cream and the Calvados or brandy, then add salt and pepper to taste. Heat the mixture over a low heat, stirring well, and taking care that the mixture does not boil. Pour this sauce over the partridges and apples, and sprinkle with chopped parsley before serving.

SERVES TWO

MRS BEETON'S TIP

Calvados is a French brandy made by distilling cider. It is a speciality of the Pays d'Auge.

PHEASANT WITH MUSHROOM STUFFING

2 pheasants
½ onion
50 g / 2 oz butter

MUSHROOM STUFFING
25 g / 1 oz butter or margarine
100 g / 4 oz finely chopped onion
100 g / 4oz mushrooms, chopped
50 g / 2 oz cooked ham, chopped
75 g / 3 oz fresh white breadcrumbs
salt and pepper
15 ml / 1 tbsp game or chicken stock (optional)
watercress sprigs, to garnish

Wash the pheasant giblets. Place in a saucepan and cover with cold water. Add the half onion and simmer gently for 40 minutes to make stock for the gravy.

Make the stuffing. Melt the butter or margarine in a frying pan and cook the onion until soft. Add the mushrooms to the onion; cook for a few minutes. Stir in the ham and breadcrumbs, then add salt and pepper. If the stuffing is too crumbly, add the stock.

Set the oven at 190°C / 375°F / gas 5. Divide the stuffing between the birds, filling the body cavities only. Truss the birds neatly and put them in a roasting tin; spread with the butter. Roast for 45–60 minutes, depending on the size of the birds. Baste occasionally while roasting. Transfer the birds to a heated serving dish and remove the trussing strings. Garnish with watercress and serve with gravy made from the giblet stock (see page 142). Wild mushrooms, tossed in butter, are good with this dish.

SERVES SIX

ORANGE-SCENTED BRAISED VENISON

1–1.25 kg / 2¼–2¾ lb haunch or shoulder of venison
25 g / 1 oz dripping
1 onion, thickly sliced
2 carrots, thickly sliced
2 celery sticks, thickly sliced
1 orange
Game Stock (page 19) or Chicken Stock (page 18) (see method)
25 g / 1 oz butter
45 ml / 3 tbsp plain flour
30 ml / 2 tbsp redcurrant jelly
salt and pepper

RED WINE MARINADE

1 onion, chopped
1 carrot, chopped
1 celery stick, sliced
6–10 parsley sprigs, chopped
1 garlic clove, crushed
5 ml / 1 tsp dried thyme
1 bay leaf
6–8 peppercorns
1–2 cloves
2.5 ml / ½ tsp ground coriander
2.5 ml / ½ tsp juniper berries
250 ml / 9 fl oz chicken stock
150 ml / ¼ pint red wine
150 ml / ¼ pint oil

GARNISH

watercress sprigs
orange slices
Mrs Beeton's Forcemeat Balls (page 139)

Combine all the ingredients for the marinade in a deep dish. Stir in 150 ml / ¼ pint water and add the venison. Leave for about 12 hours or overnight, basting and turning occasionally. Dry the venison on absorbent kitchen paper and trim if required. Reserve the marinade.

Set the oven at 190°C / 375°F / gas 5. Melt the dripping in a large frying pan and brown the venison on all sides. Remove and set aside.

Add the vegetables to the fat remaining in the pan and cook briefly, then place in a large casserole. Pare off a few thin strips of rind from the orange and add to the casserole. Strain in the marinade and add enough stock just to cover the vegetables. Place the venison on top, cover with a well-greased piece of greaseproof paper and a lid. Cook for 1¼ hours. Meanwhile cream the butter and flour together in a small bowl. Set aside.

Carve the meat into slices. Arrange them on a heated serving dish and keep hot. Strain the stock from the casserole into a small saucepan, discarding the vegetables. Squeeze the orange and strain the juice into the pan. Add the redcurrant jelly, salt and pepper, and bring to the boil. Lower the heat and stir until the jelly has melted, then add knobs of the prepared butter and flour paste, whisking well after each addition. Simmer for 2–3 minutes, whisking.

Pour the sauce over the venison and garnish with the watercress, orange slices and forcemeat balls. Serve at once.

SERVES SIX TO EIGHT

MRS BEETON'S TIP

Instead of braising a whole joint of venison, the same ingredients and method may be used for steaks. Alternatively, the joint may be cut into serving portions before cooking.

ROAST VENISON WITH BAKED APPLES

4 small sharp cooking apples
juice of 1 lemon
30 ml / 2 tbsp gooseberry, rowanberry or redcurrant jelly
15 ml / 1 tbsp butter
10 ml / 2 tsp soft light brown sugar
1 kg / 2¼ lb young venison
about 45 ml / 3 tbsp oil

SAUCE

150 ml / ¼ pint game or beef stock
30 ml / 2 tbsp gooseberry, rowanberry or redcurrant jelly
small pinch of ground cloves
salt and pepper
10 ml / 2 tsp cornflour
30 ml / 2 tbsp sherry

Set the oven at 190°C / 375°F / gas 5. Peel and core the apples. Put them in a saucepan, add a little water and the lemon juice and simmer for 10–15 minutes. Drain and arrange in an ovenproof dish. Fill the core holes with the jelly. Top each apple with butter and brown sugar.

Put the venison in a roasting tin. Brush with 30 ml / 2 tbsp of the oil and roast for 40 minutes, basting with extra oil from time to time. Bake the apples at the same time.

Meanwhile make the sauce. Combine the stock, jelly, ground cloves, salt and pepper in a small pan. Heat gently to dissolve the jelly. In a cup, blend the cornflour with 15 ml / 1 tbsp water, add to the stock and bring to the boil, stirring all the time. Cook for 2 minutes.

Slice the meat and arrange it on a warm dish with the apples; keep both hot. Place the roasting tin over the heat, add the sauce and the sherry and stir vigorously. Strain over the meat and serve at once.

SERVES FOUR TO SIX

Meat Dishes

Beef, lamb and pork can be served on Christmas day or Sunday lunches, and there are plenty of prepare-ahead recipes here to satisfy hungry house guests. A whole glazed ham makes a brilliant centrepiece, and will yield delicious slices for sandwiches and salads after the feast.

ROAST RIBS OF BEEF WITH YORKSHIRE PUDDING

This impressive joint is also known as a standing rib roast. Ask the butcher to trim the thin ends of the bones so that the joint will stand upright. The recipe below, as in Mrs Beeton's day, uses clarified dripping for cooking, but the roast may be cooked without any additional fat, if preferred. There will be sufficient fat from the meat for basting.

2.5 kg / 5½ lb forerib of beef
50–75 g / 2–3 oz beef dripping
salt and pepper
vegetable stock or water (see method)

YORKSHIRE PUDDING
100 g / 4 oz plain flour
1 egg, beaten
150 ml / ¼ pint milk

Set the oven at 230°C / 450°F / gas 8. Wipe the meat but do not salt it. Melt 50 g / 2 oz of the dripping in a roasting tin, add the meat and quickly spoon some of the hot fat over it. Roast for 10 minutes.

Lower the oven temperature to 180°C / 350°F / gas 4. Baste the meat thoroughly, then continue to roast for a further 1¾ hours for rare meat; 2¼ hours for well-done meat. Baste frequently during cooking.

Meanwhile make the Yorkshire pudding batter. Sift the flour into a bowl and add a pinch of salt. Make a well in the centre of the flour and add the beaten egg. Stir in the milk, gradually working in the flour. Beat vigorously until the mixture is smooth and bubbly, then stir in 150 ml / ¼ pint water.

About 30 minutes before the end of the cooking time, spoon off 30 ml / 2 tbsp of the dripping and divide it between six 7.5-cm / 3-inch Yorkshire pudding tins. Place the tins in the oven for 5 minutes or until the fat is very hot, then carefully divide the batter between them. Bake above the meat for 15–20 minutes (or see Mrs Beeton's Tip).

When the beef is cooked, salt it lightly, transfer it to a warmed serving platter and keep hot. Pour off almost all the water in the roasting tin, leaving the sediment. Pour in enough vegetable stock or water to make a thin gravy, then heat to boiling point, stirring all the time. Season with salt and pepper and serve in a heated gravyboat with the roast and Yorkshire puddings.

SERVES SIX TO EIGHT

MRS BEETON'S TIP

Yorkshire pudding is traditionally cooked in a large tin below the joint, so that some of the cooking juices from the meat fall into the pudding to give it an excellent flavour. In a modern oven, this means using a rotisserie or resting the meat directly on the oven shelf. The pudding should be cooked in a large roasting tin, then cut into portions and served as a course on its own before the meat course. Gravy should be poured over the portions of pudding.

BEEF WELLINGTON

This classic Beef Wellington differs from beef en croûte in that the meat is covered with fine pâté – preferably pâté de foie gras – before it is wrapped.

800 g–1 kg / 1¾ lb–2¼ lb fillet of beef
freshly ground pepper
25 g / 1 oz butter
15 ml / 1 tbsp oil
100 g / 4 oz button mushrooms, sliced
5 ml / 1 tsp chopped fresh mixed herbs
5ml / 1 tsp chopped parsley
75 g / 3 oz fine liver pâté

PUFF PASTRY
225 g / 8 oz plain flour
2.5 ml / ½ tsp salt
225 g / 8 oz butter
3.75 ml / ¾ tsp lemon juice
beaten egg for glazing

First make the pastry. Sift the flour and salt into a mixing bowl and rub in 50 g / 2 oz of the butter. Add the lemon juice and mix to a smooth dough with cold water. Shape the remaining butter into a rectangle on greaseproof paper. Roll out the dough on a lightly floured surface into a strip a little wider than the butter and rather more than twice its length. Place the butter on one half of the pastry, fold the other half over it, and press the edges together with the rolling pin. Leave in a cool place for 15 minutes to allow the butter to harden.

Roll out the pastry into a long strip. Fold the bottom third up and the top third down, press the edges together with the rolling pin and turn the pastry so that the folded edges are on the right and left. Roll and fold again, cover and leave in a cool place for 15 minutes. Repeat this process until the pastry has been rolled out six times. Chill the pastry well between each rolling, wrapping it in cling film to prevent the surface drying out. After the final rolling, leave wrapped pastry in the refrigerator until required.

Set the oven at 230ºC / 450ºF / gas 8. Wipe, trim and tie the meat into a neat shape. Season with pepper. Melt the butter in the oil in a large frying pan, add the fillet and brown it quickly all over. Carefully transfer the fillet to a roasting tin, reserving the fat in the pan, and roast it for 10–20 minutes (for rare to medium result). Remove and cool. Leave the oven on.

Heat the fat remaining in the frying pan, add the mushrooms and fry over moderate heat for 2–3 minutes. Remove from the heat, add the herbs and leave to cool.

Roll out the pastry on a lightly floured surface to a rectangle large enough to enclose the fillet. Using a slotted spoon, transfer the mushroom mixture to one half of the pastry. Lay the beef on top and spread the pâté over the meat. Wrap the pastry around the beef to form a neat parcel, sealing the edges well. Place on a baking sheet with the join underneath. Top with leaves and/or a lattice of strips cut from the pastry trimmings, glaze with beaten egg and bake for about 30 minutes. Serve hot or cold.

SERVES SIX

VARIATION

To make individual Beef Wellingtons, use six portions of raw fillet. Wrap the portions individually, including mushrooms and pâté, bringing up the pastry sides to make neat parcels. Glaze and bake, allowing 15–20 minutes for rare beef; 25–30 minutes for medium-cooked beef.

CARBONNADE OF BEEF

Brown ale and long, slow cooking combine to make this classic, full-flavoured stew with its crunchy topping of mustard-seasoned French bread.

50 g / 2 oz butter or margarine
675 g / 1½ lb stewing steak, trimmed and cut into 4-cm / 1½-inch cubes
2 large onions, sliced
1 garlic clove, crushed
15 ml / 1 tbsp plain flour
250 ml / 9 fl oz beef stock
375 ml / 13 fl oz brown ale
salt and pepper
1 bouquet garni
pinch of grated nutmeg
pinch of soft light brown sugar
5 ml / 1 tsp red wine vinegar
6 thin slices of French bread
15 ml / 1 tbsp French mustard

Set the oven at 160°C / 325°F / gas 3. Melt the butter or margarine in a heavy-bottomed frying pan, add the beef and fry quickly until browned on all sides. Using a slotted spoon, transfer the beef to a casserole and keep hot.

Add the onions to the fat remaining in the pan and fry until lightly browned, then stir in the garlic and fry over gentle heat for 1 minute. Pour off any excess fat from the pan to leave about 15 ml / 1 tbsp.

PRESSURE COOKER TIP

Follow the recipe above, removing the open pressure cooker from the heat before adding the stock and ale. The cooker should not be more than half full. Close the cooker, bring to 15 lb pressure and cook for 20 minutes. Reduce the pressure quickly. Transfer the stew to a casserole, top with the bread slices as left, and grill until golden.

Add the flour to the onions and garlic and cook, stirring constantly, until lightly browned. Gradually stir in the stock and ale, with salt and pepper to taste. Add the bouquet garni, nutmeg, brown sugar and vinegar. Bring to the boil, then pour the liquid over the beef in the casserole. Cover and bake for 1½–2 hours or until the beef is tender. Remove the bouquet garni.

Spread the French bread slices with mustard. Arrange them, mustard side up, on top of the carbonnade, pressing them down so that they absorb the gravy. Return the casserole to the oven, uncovered, for about 15 minutes or until the bread browns slightly. Alternatively, place under a hot grill for a few minutes. Serve immediately, straight from the casserole.

SERVES SIX

CHÂTEAUBRIAND STEAK

Châteaubriand is a luxury cut, from the thickest part of the beef fillet.

1 double fillet steak, not less than
4 cm / 1½ inches thick, trimmed
melted butter
freshly ground black pepper
Maître d'Hôtel Butter (page 147) or
Béarnaise Sauce (page 153) to serve

Brush the steak generously all over with melted butter, season with pepper and place on a rack in a grill pan. Cook under a very hot grill for 2–3 minutes until browned and sealed. Turn the steak over, using a palette knife or spoons, and grill until browned. Lower the heat slightly and continue grilling, turning the steak once or twice, until cooked to taste. Rare meat will require a total cooking time of about 20 minutes; for medium-rare add an extra 5 minutes.

Cut the meat downwards at a slight angle into four even slices. Put two slices on each of two heated plates, top with Maître d'Hôtel Butter or Béarnaise Sauce and serve at once.

SERVES TWO

HERBED SHOULDER OF LAMB

This recipe maybe used for leg as well as for shoulder of lamb.

1 shoulder of lamb, boned
4 garlic cloves, peeled and quartered lengthways
about 6 small sprigs each fresh rosemary and thyme
4 bay leaves
2 oranges
60 ml / 4 tbsp olive oil
salt and pepper
300 ml / ½ pint red wine

GARNISH
orange slices
fresh herbs

Trim any lumps of fat from the lamb, then tie it in a neat shape if the butcher has not already done this. Weigh the joint and calculate the cooking time at 30 minutes per 450 g / 1 lb plus 30 minutes. Use a small pointed knife to make short cuts into the lamb, at an angle running under the skin, all over the joint. Insert pieces of garlic and the rosemary and thyme sprigs into the cuts. Place the joint in a deep dish, with two bay leaves underneath and two on top.

Pare two long strips of rind off one orange and add them to the dish, placing them next to or on top of the lamb. Squeeze the juice from the oranges, then mix it with the olive oil, salt and pepper. Pour this mixture over the lamb, cover and marinate for several hours or overnight. Turn the joint at least once during the marinating time.

Set the oven at 180°C / 350°F / gas 4. Transfer the joint to a roasting tin, adding the bay leaves and orange rind but reserving the marinade. Cook for half the calculated time, brushing occasionally with the reserved marinade and basting with cooking juices from the tin. Pour the remaining marinade and the wine over the joint and continue roasting. Baste the lamb occasionally and add a little water to the juices in the tin if they begin to dry up – if the roasting tin is large they will evaporate more speedily.

Transfer the cooked joint to a serving dish, cover with foil and set aside. Pour 300 ml / ½ pint boiling water or vegetable cooking water into the roasting tin. Boil the cooking juices rapidly, stirring and scraping the sediment off the base and sides of the pan, until they are reduced by half. Taste for seasoning, then strain the sauce into a heated sauceboat.

Garnish the lamb with orange slices and fresh herbs and serve at once, carving it into thick slices. Offer the sauce separately.

SERVES SIX

MRS BEETON'S TIP

Once it has been reduced, the sauce may be thickened by whisking in small knobs of beurre manié, then boiling for 2 minutes, whisking all the time. To make beurre manié cream 25 g / 1 oz butter with 30–45 ml / 2–3 tbsp plain flour.

LOIN OF LAMB WITH LEMON AND PARSLEY STUFFING

Adapted from one of Mrs Beeton's first edition recipes for a loin of mutton, this lightly spiced roast joint was originally part baked and part stewed. It was justifiably described as 'very excellent'. The same combination of ingredients and stuffing will complement a leg or shoulder joint.

1 x 1.4–1.6 kg / 3–3½ lb boned and rolled double loin of lamb, bones reserved, trimmed
salt and pepper
1.25 ml / ¼ tsp each ground allspice and mace, and grated nutmeg
6 cloves
600 ml / 1 pint lamb, Chicken (page 18) or Vegetable Stock (page 20)
30 ml / 2 tbsp plain flour
25 g / 1 oz butter
125 ml / 4 fl oz port
30 ml / 2 tbsp mushroom ketchup
100 g / 4 oz button mushrooms, sliced

LEMON AND PARSLEY STUFFING
50 g / 2 oz shredded beef suet
50 g / 2 oz cooked ham, chopped
15 ml / 1 tbsp finely chopped parsley
5 ml / 1 tsp chopped fresh thyme
grated rind of ½ lemon
175 g / 6 oz fresh white breadcrumbs
2.5 ml / ½ tsp grated nutmeg or ground mace
pinch of cayenne pepper
1 egg, beaten
a little milk

Open out the lamb and sprinkle the inside lightly with salt and pepper. Mix the allspice, mace and nutmeg, then rub the spices all over the meat, both outside and on the cut surface. Cover and allow to marinate for at least 1 hour, or up to 24 hours.

Make the stuffing. Combine the suet, ham, parsley, thyme, lemon rind, breadcrumbs and nutmeg or mace in a bowl. Add salt and pepper to taste, and the cayenne. Stir in the egg and add enough milk to bind the mixture lightly together. Spread the stuffing evenly over the inside of the lamb, carefully roll it up again and tie it neatly. Stick the cloves into the joint, piercing it first with the point of a knife.

Set the oven at 180°C / 350°F / gas 4. Put the lamb bones in the bottom of a roasting tin and pour over just enough stock to cover them. Weigh the meat and calculate the cooking time. Allow 30 minutes per 450 g / 1 lb plus 30 minutes over. Place the stuffed lamb on top of the bones in the tin. Cook for the calculated time, adding extra stock or water during cooking to maintain the level of liquid just below the top of the bones and. joint. Baste the joint occasionally with the cooking juices.

When the lamb is cooked, transfer it to a heated serving platter and allow to rest under tented foil. Remove the bones and skim off most of the fat from the liquid in the roasting tin. Beat the flour and butter to a smooth paste. Place the roasting liquid over medium heat, stir in the port and mushroom ketchup, then bring the mixture to simmering point. Whisking all the time, gradually add small lumps of the butter and flour mixture. Continue whisking well after each addition, until the sauce boils and thickens. Stir in the mushrooms and simmer for 3 minutes.

Taste the sauce for seasoning before serving it with the lamb, which should be carved into thick slices. Redcurrant jelly, new potatoes and fresh peas are excellent accompaniments.

SERVES SIX

ROAST RACK OF LAMB

1 rack of lamb
45 ml / 3 tbsp plain flour
salt and pepper
30 ml / 2 tbsp redcurrant jelly

Set the oven at 180°C / 350°F / gas 4. Weigh the joint of lamb and calculate the cooking time at 25 minutes per 450 g / 1 lb, plus 25 minutes. This gives a medium result; for a well-done joint allow 30 minutes per 450 g / 1 lb plus 30 minutes.

Dust the joint with flour and plenty of seasoning. Place it in a roasting tin and cook for three-quarters of the time, basting occasionally. Pour off excess fat and pour in 600 ml / 1 pint boiling water. Finish roasting the meat.

Meanwhile, melt the jelly in a small saucepan. Transfer the meat to a serving plate and glaze it with the jelly. Tent with foil to keep hot. Boil the cooking liquor until reduced by about a third, taste for seasoning, pour into a gravyboat and serve with the lamb.

SERVES FOUR TO SIX

VARIATIONS

- **Crown Roast or Guard of Honour** A pair of racks of lamb may be trussed into a crown roast or a guard of honour. For a crown, the racks are sewn end to end, then trussed (sewn) into a ring with the fat side inwards and trimmed bones forming the top of the crown. For a guard of honour, the racks are arranged opposite each other with bone ends interlocked. Both joints are sold ready prepared; both may be stuffed. Stuffing is spooned into the middle of the crown roast or packed between the racks for a guard of honour.

LAMB CUTLETS EN PAPILLOTE

oil for greasing
4–6 slices of cooked ham
6 lamb cutlets, trimmed
15 ml / 1 tbsp oil
1 onion, finely chopped
25 g / 1 oz button mushrooms, finely chopped
10 ml / 2 tsp finely chopped parsley
grated rind of ½ lemon
salt and pepper

Set the oven at 190°C / 375°F / gas 5. Cut out 12 small rounds of ham, each large enough to cover the round part of a cutlet. Heat the oil in a small saucepan and fry the onion for 4–6 minutes until slightly softened. Remove from the heat and stir in the mushrooms, parsley and lemon rind, with salt and pepper to taste. Leave to cool.

Cut out six heart-shaped pieces of double thickness greaseproof paper or foil large enough to hold the cutlets. Grease the paper generously with oil. Centre one of the ham rounds on the right half of one of the prepared paper hearts, spread with a little of the mushroom mixture and lay a cutlet on top. Spread the cutlet with a little more of the mushroom mixture and add another round of ham so that the round part of the cutlet is neatly sandwiched. Fold over the paper and twist the edges well together.

Lay the wrapped cutlets on a greased baking sheet and bake for 30 minutes. Transfer, still in their wrappings, to heated individual plates and serve at once.

SERVES SIX

ROAST PORK WITH MUSHROOM AND CORN STUFFING

If the whole joint is taken to the table, you may like to add a garnish of baby sweetcorn cobs (cook them in boiling water for 3–5 minutes) and button mushrooms tossed in hot butter.

1.5 kg / 3¼ lb boned bladebone of pork, scored
(see Mrs Beeton's Tip)
45 ml / 3 tbsp oil
15 ml / 1 tbsp cooking salt

MUSHROOM AND CORN STUFFING
25 g / 1 oz butter or margarine
1 onion, finely chopped
1 celery stick, finely chopped
100 g / 4 oz mushrooms, finely chopped
50 g / 2 oz thawed frozen sweetcorn, drained
50 g / 2 oz fresh white breadcrumbs
15 ml / 1 tbsp chopped parsley
2.5 ml / ½ tsp ground mace
5 ml / 1 tsp lemon juice
salt and pepper

Set the oven at 230°C / 450°F / gas 8. Make the stuffing. Melt the butter or margarine in a small saucepan, then add the onion and celery and fry for 4–6 minutes until soft but not browned. Remove from the heat and add the remaining ingredients.

Spoon the stuffing evenly into the 'pocket' left when the meat was boned. Roll up the joint and tie with thin string at regular intervals. Generously brush 15 ml / 1 tbsp of the oil over the rind. Sprinkle with the salt, rubbing it well in.

Heat the remaining oil in a roasting tin, add the meat, turning it in the hot fat, and roast for 20–30 minutes until the crackling crisps. Do not cover the meat or the crackling will soften again. Lower the heat to 180°C / 350°F / gas 4 and cook for about 1½ hours more or until the pork is cooked.

Transfer the meat to a warmed serving dish, remove the string and keep hot. If liked, pour off the fat from the roasting tin, using the sediment for gravy (see page 142).

SERVES SIX

MRS BEETON'S TIP

If the butcher has not already scored the pork rind, do this yourself, using a very sharp knife and making the cuts about 3 mm / ⅛ inch deep and 1 cm / ½ inch apart.

LOIN OF PORK STUFFED WITH PRUNES

1.25–1.5 kg / 2¾–3¼ lb boned loin of pork
200 g / 7 oz ready-to-eat prunes
juice of 1 lemon
salt and pepper

Set the oven at 180°C / 350°F / gas 4. Weigh the meat and calculate the cooking time at 30 minutes per 450 g / 1 lb plus 30 minutes over. Spread the prunes over the pork flesh, roll up the meat and tie it securely. Pour the lemon juice all over the meat, rubbing it well in.

Put the meat in a roasting tin, season with salt and pepper and roast for the calculated cooking time, basting occasionally. Serve on a heated platter, accompanied with a thickened gravy made from the sediment in the roasting tin (see page 142).

SERVES SIX

SAVOURY LOIN OF PORK

1–1.5 kg / 2¼–3¼ lb loin of pork on the bone
15 ml / 1 tbsp finely chopped onion
2.5 ml / ½ tsp dried sage
2.5 ml / ½ tsp salt
1.25 ml / ¼ tsp freshly ground pepper
pinch of dry mustard
30 ml / 2 tbsp sieved apricot jam, melted
125 ml / 4 fl oz Apple Sauce (page 148)

Set the oven at 220°C / 425°F / gas 7. Weigh the meat and calculate the cooking time at 30 minutes per 450 g / 1 lb plus 30 minutes over. Mix the onion, sage, salt, pepper and mustard in a small bowl. Rub the mixture well into the surface of the meat.

Put the meat in a roasting tin and roast for 10 minutes, then lower the oven temperature to 180°C / 350°F / gas 4 and roast for the remainder of the calculated cooking time. About 30 minutes before serving, remove the pork from the oven and brush with melted apricot jam. Continue cooking to crisp the crackling.

Serve the pork on a heated serving dish, offering the Apple Sauce separately.

SERVES SIX

MRS BEETON'S TIP

If a savoury glaze is preferred for the crackling, brush with oil and sprinkle with salt. Raise the oven temperature to 220°C / 425°F / gas 7, return the pork to the oven and continue cooking for 15–20 minutes.

ROAST PORK WITH SAGE AND ONION STUFFING

Use the pan juices from the pork to make a gravy and offer Apple Sauce (page 148) as an accompaniment.

4 large onions
100 g / 4 oz fresh breadcrumbs
45 ml / 3 tbsp chopped fresh sage or 15 ml / 1 tbsp dried sage
salt and pepper
40 g / 1½ oz butter, melted
1 egg
1. 5 kg / 3¼ lb boned joint from leg of pork, boned and scored
30 ml / 2 tbsp oil

Place the onions in a saucepan, cover with water and bring to the boil. Cook for 5 minutes, then drain, cool slightly and chop. Mix the onions with the breadcrumbs. Add the sage, plenty of seasoning, the butter and the egg.

Set the oven at 180°C / 350°F / gas 4. Make sure the pork rind is well scored. Fill the cavity left by the bone with some stuffing, then tie the joint into a neat shape. Place the remaining stuffing in a buttered, ovenproof dish; set aside.

Place the joint in a roasting tin and rub plenty of salt into the rind, then trickle the oil over. Roast for about 2 hours, basting the joint occasionally, until cooked through. Place the dish of stuffing in the oven halfway through cooking.

SERVES SIX

HONEY-GLAZED HAM

1.5–2 kg / 3¼–4½ lb ham
500 ml / 18 fl oz dry cider
5 ml / 1 tsp prepared mustard
45 ml / 3 tbsp set honey
generous pinch of ground cloves
1 x 227 g / 8 oz can pineapple chunks, drained, juice reserved
maraschino cherries, halved
20 ml / 4 tsp softened butter
15 ml / 1 tbsp double cream
watercress sprigs, to garnish

Parboil the ham for 20 minutes per 450 g / 1 lb, then drain and place in a large baking tin. Set the oven at 180°C / 350°F / gas 4.

Pour the cider over the ham, cover the tin tightly with foil and bake for 30 minutes. Meanwhile make the glaze by mixing the mustard, honey and ground cloves together in a small bowl.

When the ham is cooked, lift it out of the tin, reserving the juices in a measuring jug. Remove the rind and score the fat into a diamond pattern. Brush generously with about half the honey glaze. Place pineapple chunks and halved cherries, cut side down, in alternate diamonds on the ham. Brush with a little more glaze, taking care not to disturb the garnish. Return the ham to the tin and bake, loosely covered with foil, for about 20 minutes or until the glaze is set.

Meanwhile add the reserved pineapple juice to the cooking juices. Make up to 600 ml / 1 pint with water, if necessary. Pour into a small saucepan and bring to simmering point. Add the butter, in small pieces, stirring after each addition until melted. Simmer until well reduced and flavoured, then remove from the heat, add the cream and pour into a heated sauceboat. Garnish the ham with watercress and serve hot, with the sauce. The sauce may be omitted, and the ham served cold, if preferred.

SERVES EIGHT TO TEN

VARIATION

- **Marmalade Glaze** Heat 250 ml / 9 fl oz marmalade with 30 ml / 2 tbsp cider vinegar and 30 ml / 2 tbsp orange juice. Use as suggested above. Instead of studding the ham with pineapple and cherries, use thin slices of sweet orange, secured with cloves.

BAKED HAM LOAF

oil for greasing
100 g / 4 oz dried breadcrumbs
350 g / 12 oz cooked ham, minced
50 g / 2 oz sultanas
1 large cooking apple
15 ml / 1 tbsp chopped parsley
5 ml / 1 tsp grated lemon rind
pinch of ground allspice
pinch of grated nutmeg
salt and pepper
2 eggs, beaten
milk (see method)

Grease a 450-g / 1-lb loaf tin and coat it with some of the breadcrumbs. Set the oven at 150°C / 300°F / gas 2.

Put the remaining breadcrumbs in a mixing bowl and add the minced ham and sultanas. Peel, core and grate the apple. Add it to the bowl with the parsley, lemon rind, spices, and salt and pepper to taste. Bind with the beaten eggs, adding a little milk if necessary.

Spoon the mixture into the prepared tin, taking care not to disturb the bread-crumb coating. Bake for 40 minutes. Allow to cool for 5 minutes, then turn out on to a heated serving dish. Serve hot, or cold.

SERVES SIX

MEATLOAF

oil for greasing
450 g / 1 lb minced beef or pork, or a mixture of both
50 g / 2 oz fresh breadcrumbs
1 large onion, finely chopped
30 ml / 2 tbsp chopped parsley
5 ml / 1 tsp chopped fresh thyme
5 ml / 1 tsp chopped fresh sage
1 egg
15 ml / 1 tbsp Worcestershire sauce
salt and pepper

Grease a 450-g / 1-lb loaf tin. Set the oven at 180°C / 350°F / gas 4. Place all the ingredients in a bowl, adding plenty of salt and pepper. Pound the ingredients with the back of a mixing spoon until thoroughly combined and well bound together.

Turn the mixture into the tin, press it down well and cover the top with a piece of greased greaseproof paper. Bake for 1 hour, until firm and shrunk away from the tin slightly. Turn out and serve hot or cold.

SERVES FOUR

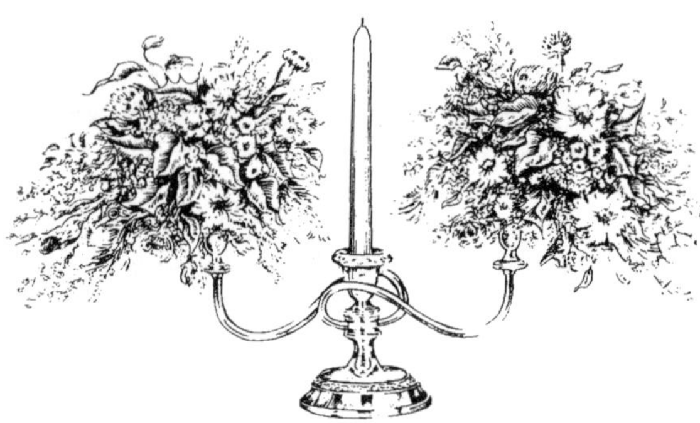

Fish Dishes

An entire poached salmon, attractively garnished, creates an impact at any party. Included here are recipes you can serve hot or cold for large numbers of people, Kedgeree for relaxed brunches and a tasty way of frying fish for a fast, light supper.

HOT POACHED SALMON

Court Bouillon is the traditional cooking liquid for poached fish and is discarded after use. Serve hot poached salmon with Hollandaise Sauce (page 152). Cold poached salmon may be garnished with cucumber slices. See Garnishing Salmon, page 94.

1 x 1.6–3.25 kg / 3½–7 lb salmon

COURT BOUILLON

1 litre / 1¾ pints dry white wine or dry cider
60 ml / 4 tbsp white wine vinegar
4 large carrots, sliced
4 large onions, sliced
4–5 celery sticks, chopped
12 parsley stalks. crushed
1 bouquet garni
20 peppercorns, lightly crushed
salt and pepper

First make the Court Bouillon. Put the wine in a large stainless steel or enamel saucepan. Add 2 litres / 3½ pints water, with the remaining ingredients. Bring to the boil, lower the heat and simmer for 30 minutes. Cool, then strain.

Cut the fins from the fish, remove the scales and thoroughly wash the body cavity. Tie the mouth of the fish shut. Tie the body of the fish loosely to keep it in shape during cooking – two or three bands of string around the fish to prevent the body cavity from gaping are usually sufficient. Weigh the fish and calculate the cooking time. Allow 5 minutes per 450 g / 1 lb for salmon up to 2.25 kg / 5 lb in weight; 4 minutes per 450 g / 1 lb plus 5 minutes for salmon up to 3.25 kg / 7 lb.

Put the fish in a fish kettle and pour over the Court Bouillon. Bring the liquid gently to just below boiling point. Lower the heat and simmer for the required cooking time. The court bouillon should barely show signs of simmering; if the liquid is allowed to bubble then it may damage the delicate salmon flesh. If serving the salmon cold, simmer for 5 minutes only, then leave the fish to cool in the cooking liquid.

Drain the salmon well and untie the body. Slide the salmon on to a large, heated platter. Slit the skin around the body immediately below the head and just above the tail of the fish. Carefully peel back the skin from the head towards the tail. Carefully turn the fish over and remove the skin from the second side. Remove the string from the mouth.

Garnish the salmon with lemon slices and parsley sprigs. Freshly cooked vegetables (new potatoes and baby carrots) may be arranged around the fish. Serve at once.

SERVINGS FROM SALMON

Hot salmon served as a main course will yield the following servings. Served cold and dressed, as part of a buffet with other main dishes, it will yield about 2 extra portions.

1.6 kg / 3½ lb salmon	4 portions
2.25 kg / 5 lb salmon	6 portions
3.25 kg / 7 lb salmon	10 portions

BONING POACHED SALMON

Follow the recipe for Hot Poached Salmon opposite. Cool the fish in the court bouillon, following the instructions for serving cold and removing the skin.

MICROWAVE TIP

Provided it can be curled into a circular dish that will fit into your microwave, salmon may be cooked by this method. Prepare the fish, tuck 2 bay leaves, some peppercorns and a small sprig of parsley into the body cavity, then curl the fish into the dish (a 25 cm / 10 inch quiche dish works well). Cover fish and dish with two layers of microwave-proof film to hold the fish securely and prevent it from losing its shape. Cook on High. A 2.25 kg / 5 lb salmon will take about 12 minutes. If you do not have a turntable turn the dish three times while cooking. Allow to stand, covered, for 5 minutes. To serve hot, drain, remove the herbs from the body cavity and skin as suggested above. Allow to cool in the wrapping if serving cold.

Using a sharp, pointed knife, cut the flesh around the head down to the bone. Cut the flesh down to the bone around the tail. Make a cut into the flesh along the length of the fish as far as the bone (above).

Cut horizontally into the flesh, along the backbone of the fish, from head to tail to loosen the top fillet.

Have a piece of foil on the work surface beside the fish ready to hold the fillets. You need a long palette knife or two fish slices to remove the fillet. Carefully slide the knife or slices under the fillet and lift it off in one piece. If the fish is large, cut the fillet in half or into three portions, then remove each piece neatly.

Carefully cut the flesh off the bone over the belly of the fish and lift it off, in one piece or several pieces, as before.

Now remove all the bones from the fish. If serving a salmon trout, snip the backbone at the head and tail end. The bones of salmon come away easily in sections.

When all the bones have been removed, carefully replace the fillets in their original position. There will be small gaps and untidy-looking areas but these will be covered by the garnish.

If the fish has been curved for cooking, it should be garnished with the bones in place.

GARNISHING SALMON

The final dressing: cut the finest possible slices of cucumber. Thick slices will not do – they have to be thin enough to curve to the shape of the fish. Dip each slice in lemon juice and lay it on the salmon. Start at the tail, overlapping each row of cucumber to mimic scales.

Pipe mayonnaise stars or shells around the tail and head of the fish, also along the top and base of the body if liked. Small triangles of lemon slices or sliced stuffed olives may be used to cover the eye of the fish. Sprigs of parsley may also be used as a garnish.

KEDGEREE

No Victorian country-house breakfast would have been complete without kedgeree. Hard-boiled egg and parsley are the traditional garnish, sometimes arranged in the shape of the cross of St Andrew.

salt and pepper
150 g / 5 oz long-grain rice
125 ml / 4 fl oz milk
450 g / 1 lb smoked haddock
50 g / 2 oz butter
15 ml / 1 tbsp curry powder
2 hard-boiled eggs, roughly chopped
cayenne pepper to taste

GARNISH
15 g / ½ oz butter
1 hard-boiled egg, white and yolk sieved separately
15 ml / 1 tbsp chopped parsley

Bring a saucepan of salted water to the boil. Add the rice and cook for 12 minutes. Drain thoroughly, rinse under cold water and drain again. Place the strainer over a saucepan of simmering water to keep the rice warm.

Put the milk in a large shallow pan with 125 ml / 4 fl oz water. Bring to simmering point, add the fish and poach gently for 4 minutes. Using a slotted spoon and a fish slice, transfer the haddock to a wooden board. Discard the cooking liquid. Remove the skin and any bones from the haddock and break up the flesh into fairly large flakes. Melt half the butter in a large saucepan. Blend in the curry powder and add the flaked fish. Warm the mixture through. Remove from the heat, lightly stir in the chopped eggs; add salt, pepper and cayenne.

Melt the remaining butter in a second pan, add the rice and toss until well coated. Add salt, pepper and cayenne. Add the rice to the haddock mixture and mix well. Pile the kedgeree on to a warmed dish. Dot the kedgeree with the butter, garnish with sieved hard-boiled egg yolk, egg white and parsley and serve at once.

SERVES FOUR

KOULIBIAC

Koulibiac is a large oblong pastry from Russia filled with a mixture of cooked rice and salmon. Smoked salmon offcuts or canned salmon may be used instead of fresh salmon. Instead of following the method described below, cook the fish on a covered plate which fits tightly over the saucepan, if preferred. This is good either hot or cold and is therefore ideal for formal meals, buffets or picnics.

butter for greasing
450 g / 1 lb salmon fillet or steaks
salt and pepper
juice of ½ lemon
175 g / 6 oz long-grain rice
50 g / 2 oz butter
1 onion, chopped
60 ml / 4 tbsp chopped parsley
4 hard-boiled eggs, roughly chopped
15 ml / 1 tbsp chopped fresh tarragon (optional)
450g / 1 lb Puff Pastry (page 74)
1 egg, beaten, to glaze
150 ml / ¼ pint soured cream to serve

Lay the salmon on a piece of greased foil large enough to enclose it completely. Sprinkle with salt, pepper and a little of the lemon juice, then wrap the foil around the fish, sealing the edges.

Place the rice in a large saucepan and add 450 ml / ¾ pint water. Bring to the boil, lower the heat and cover the pan. Simmer the rice for 10 minutes, then place the foil-wrapped fish on top of the rice. Cover the pan again and cook for about 10 minutes more or until the grains of rice are tender and all the water has been absorbed.

At the end of the cooking time, remove the foil-packed salmon from the pan. Transfer the fish to a board, reserving all the cooking juices, then discard the skin and any bones. Coarsely flake the flesh and set the fish aside. Tip the cooked rice into a bowl.

Melt half the butter in a small saucepan. Add the onion and cook over low heat for about 15 minutes until it is soft but not browned. Mix the cooked onion with the rice and add the salmon and parsley, with salt and pepper to taste. Put the chopped hard-boiled eggs in a bowl. Stir in the remaining lemon juice and add the tarragon, if used. Melt the remaining butter and trickle it over the eggs.

Set the oven at 220°C / 425°F / gas 7. Cut a large sheet of foil, at least 30 cm / 12 inches long. On a floured board, roll out the pastry to a rectangle measuring about 50 x 25 cm / 20 x 10 inches. Trim the pastry to 43 x 25 cm / 17 x 10 inches. Cut the trimmings into long narrow strips. Set aside.

Lay the pastry on the foil. Spoon half the rice mixture lengthways down the middle of the pastry. Top with the egg mixture in an even layer, then mound the remaining mixture over the top. Fold one long side of pastry over the filling and brush the edge with beaten egg. Fold the other side over and press the long edges together firmly. Brush the inside of the pastry at the ends with egg and seal them firmly.

Use the foil to turn the koulibiac over so that the pastry seam is underneath, then lift it on to a baking sheet or roasting tin. Brush all over with beaten egg and arrange the reserved strips of pastry in a lattice pattern over the top. Brush these with egg too.

Bake the koulibiac for 30–40 minutes, until the pastry is well puffed and golden. Check after 25 minutes and if the pastry looks well browned, tent a piece of foil over the top to prevent it from overcooking.

Serve in thick slices with a small dish of soured cream.

SERVES EIGHT

FRENCH FRIED HADDOCK

1 kg / 2¼ lb haddock fillets, skinned
250 ml / 9 fl oz milk
100 g / 4 oz plain flour
salt and pepper
oil for deep frying
lemon wedges, to serve

Cut the fish into 4–5 portions. Pour the milk into a shallow bowl. Spread out the flour in a second bowl; add salt and pepper. Dip the pieces of fish first into milk and then into flour, shaking off the excess.

Put the oil for frying into a deep wide pan. Heat the oil to 180–190°C / 350–375°F or until a cube of bread added to the oil browns in 30 seconds. If using a deep-fat fryer, follow the manufacturer's instructions.

Carefully lower the fish into the hot oil and fry for 3–5 minutes until evenly browned. Drain on absorbent kitchen paper and serve on a warmed platter, with lemon wedges.

SERVES FOUR TO FIVE

VARIATION

All fish fillets can be cooked by this method.

MRS BEETON'S TIP

The fish should be of uniform thickness for frying. Any thin pieces, such as tail ends, should be folded double before flouring the fish.

Vegetarian Main Courses

Tasty nut roast makes a popular vegetarian Christmas dinner, but why not try a bake with protein-rich pulses, cheese fondue to generate an instant party atmosphere, or vegetarian lasagne using festive Stilton.

NUT ROAST

The mixture for this delicious nut roast can be prepared ahead.

oil for frying and roasting
1 onion, finely chopped
2 cloves garlic, crushed
6 medium mushrooms, sliced
15 ml / 1 tbsp plain flour, plus extra for coating
300 ml / ½ pint Vegetable Stock (page 20)
175 g / 6 oz finely chopped unsalted, unroasted nuts
175 g / 6 oz breadcrumbs
1 tbsp soy or chilli sauce
2.5 ml / ½ tsp dried herbs or
30 ml / 2 tbsp fresh herbs
salt and pepper to taste

Set the oven at 190°C / 375°F / gas 5. Fry the onion over a moderate heat in about a tablespoon of oil for 5 minutes or until soft and transparent. Add the garlic and mushrooms. Cook until the mushrooms have released their juice.

Stir in the flour. Slowly pour in the stock, stirring continuously. Bring to the boil, and simmer gently for 5 minutes. Stir in the nuts, breadcrumbs, soy or chilli sauce, herbs and seasoning.

Turn the mixture on to a floured board and shape into a loaf. Heat about a tablespoon of oil in a roasting tin in the oven. Dust the loaf with flour, place in the tin and bake for 40 minutes, basting occasionally.

SERVES FOUR

BOSTON ROAST

butter for greasing
300 g / 11 oz haricot beans, soaked overnight in cold water to cover
salt and pepper
15 ml / 1 tbsp oil
1 onion, chopped
150 g / 5 oz Cheddar cheese, grated
60 ml / 4 tbsp vegetable stock
1 egg, beaten
100 g / 4oz fresh white breadcrumbs
5 ml / 1 tsp dried thyme
2.5 ml / ½ tsp grated nutmeg

Drain the beans, put them in a saucepan and add fresh water to cover. Do not add salt. Bring to the boil, cook for 10 minutes, then lower the heat and simmer for about 40 minutes or until tender. Drain the beans. Mash with seasoning or purée in a food processor.

Set the oven at 180°C / 350°F / gas 4. Heat the oil in a frying pan, add the onion and fry for about 10 minutes, or until softened. Tip the onion into a large bowl and add the mashed or puréed beans with the rest of the ingredients.

Spoon the mixture into a well greased 900-g / 2-lb loaf tin. Cover the surface with greased greaseproof paper. Bake for 45 minutes, until firm and slightly shrunk. Serve with Tomato Sauce (page 151).

SERVES SIX

FREEZER TIP

Boston Roast freezes very well. Cool quickly, then slice. Separate individual slices with freezer film and wrap in an airtight polythene bag.

LENTIL AND STILTON LASAGNE

225 g / 8 oz green lentils
8 sheets of lasagne
salt and pepper
30 ml / 2 tbsp olive oil
1 large onion, chopped
1 garlic clove, crushed
5 ml / 1 tsp dried marjoram
225 g / 8 oz mushrooms, sliced
2 x 397 g / 14 oz cans chopped tomatoes
225 g / 8 oz ripe blue Stilton cheese (without rind)
30 ml / 2 tbsp plain flour
300 ml / ½ pint milk

Cook the lentils in plenty of boiling water for 35 minutes, until just tender. Cook the lasagne sheets in boiling salted waterwith a little oil added for 12–15 minutes, or until just tender. Drain both and set the lentils aside; lay the lasagne out to dry on absorbent kitchen paper.

Heat the remaining oil in a large saucepan. Add the onion, garlic and marjoram and cook for 10 minutes until just soft. Add the mushrooms, cook for 5 minutes then add the tomatoes. Stir in the lentils with plenty of salt and pepper and bring to the boil. Reduce the heat and cover the pan, then simmer for 5 minutes.

Set the oven at 180°C / 350°F / gas 4. Grease a lasagne dish or large ovenproof dish. Pour in half the lentil mixture and top it with half the lasagne. Pour the remaining lentil mixture over the pasta, then end with the remaining pasta.

Mash the Stilton in a bowl with a fork or process it in a food processor. Sprinkle a little of the flour over the cheese and work it in, then add the remaining flour in the same way so the mixture is crumbly. Gradually add the milk, a little at a time, pounding the cheese at first, then beating it as it softens. When the mixture is soft and creamy, the remaining milk may be incorporated more quickly. Add some pepper and just a little salt. Pour the mixture over the lasagne, scraping the bowl clean. Bake in the preheated oven for 40–45 minutes, or until the top of the lasagne is well browned and bubbling.

SERVES SIX

VARIATION

- **Lentil and Leek Lasagne** Omit the onion in the main recipe and use 450 g / 1 lb sliced leeks. Cook them with an additional knob of butter until well reduced. Continue as above. Cheddar may be substituted for the Stilton: it should be finely grated or chopped in a food processor.

SWISS CHEESE FONDUE

Cheese fondue is traditionally made in an open ceramic or earthenware pan called a caquelon. *The pan is set over a spirit lamp or burner and long-handled fondue forks enable each guest to spear a cube of bread and dip it into the fondue mixture. The golden crust which forms in the bottom of the pan is a traditional, end-of-fondue treat.*

1 garlic clove
300 ml / ½ pint light dry white wine
350 g / 12 oz Emmental cheese, grated
450 g / 1 lb Gruyère cheese, grated
10 ml / 2 tsp cornflour or potato flour
15 ml / 1 tbsp kirsch
white pepper and grated nutmeg
2 long French sticks, cubed

Cut the garlic clove in half and rub the cut sides over the inside of a fondue pan or flameproof casserole. Pour the wine into the pan or casserole and heat until steaming, but not simmering. Gradually add the grated cheese, a little at a time, stirring constantly. Allow each addition of cheese to melt before adding the next. Remove the pan from the heat.

Mix the cornflour or potato flour to a paste with the kirsch and stir this into the fondue. Return to the heat and cook, stirring constantly, until the mixture is smooth, thick and creamy. Add pepper and nutmeg to taste. Set the pan over a burner or hotplate at the table. Serve at once, with the bread.

SERVES SIX TO EIGHT

SOYA BEAN BAKE

butter or oil for greasing
450 g / 1 lb soya beans, soaked for 24 hours in cold water to cover
2 onions, finely chopped
1 green pepper, seeded and chopped
1 carrot, coarsely grated
1 celery stick, sliced
45 ml / 3 tbsp molasses
45 ml / 3 tbsp chopped parsley
5 ml / 1 tsp dried thyme
5 ml / 1 tsp dried savory or marjoram
salt and pepper
2 x 397 g / 14 oz cans chopped tomatoes
175 g / 6 oz medium oatmeal
50 g / 2 oz Lancashire or Caerphilly cheese, finely crumbled or grated
45 ml / 3 tbsp snipped chives
50 ml / 2 fl oz olive oil

Grease a large ovenproof dish – a lasagne dish is ideal. Set the oven at 180°C / 350°F / gas 4. Drain the beans. Put them in a saucepan with fresh water to cover. Bring to the boil and boil vigorously for 45 minutes. Lower the heat, add more boiling water if necessary, cover the pan and simmer for 1½–2 hours until tender. Top up the water as necessary.

Drain the beans and put them in a mixing bowl with the onions, green pepper, carrot and celery. Warm the molasses in a small saucepan and pour it over the bean mixture. Stir in the herbs and season with salt and pepper. Mix in the canned tomatoes.

Spoon the mixture into the prepared dish. Mix together the oatmeal, cheese and chives. Spoon the oatmeal mixture over the beans, then drizzle the olive oil over the top. Cover the dish with foil or a lid and bake for 45 minutes. Remove the lid and bake for a further 15 minutes. Serve hot, from the dish.

SERVES SIX

Side Dishes

Roast potatoes and parsnips, chestnuts and Brussels sprouts, carrots and cauliflower cheese are popular accompaniments to Christmas dinner. There are many other appetizing vegetable dishes here to introduce colour and variety to any table.

ROAST POTATOES

6 large potatoes, peeled and quartered
120 ml / 8 tbsp vegetable or olive oil, goose or duck fat or other fat reserved for roasting
pinch of salt

Place the potatoes in a large saucepan and just cover with cold water. Bring to the boil then boil, uncovered, for 5 minutes.

Meanwhile, switch the oven to 220°C / 425°F / gas mark 7 and place the oil or fat in a large roasting tin towards the top of the oven to heat thoroughly. Drain the potatoes thoroughly (reserving the water for gravy, stock or soup). Return them to the pan in batches and shake vigorously to soften the edges, or you can scratch them with a fork.

Take the tin from the oven and add the potatoes. Turn them quickly in the oil then cook at the top of the oven for 50-60 minutes, turning once halfway through cooking until crisp and golden on the outside and soft in the centre. Drain and sprinkle with salt. Serve as soon as possible.

SERVES 4

DUCHESSE POTATOES

butter or margarine for greasing
450 g / 1 lb old potatoes
salt and pepper
25 g / 1 oz butter or margarine
1 egg or 2 egg yolks
grated nutmeg (optional)
beaten egg for brushing

Grease a baking sheet. Cut the potatoes into pieces and cook in a saucepan of salted water for 15–20 minutes. Drain thoroughly, then press the potatoes through a sieve into a large mixing bowl.

Set the oven at 200°C / 400°F / gas 6. Beat the butter or margarine and egg or egg yolks into the potatoes. Add salt and pepper to taste and the nutmeg, if used. Spoon the mixture into a piping bag fitted with a large rose nozzle. Pipe rounds of potato on to the prepared baking sheet. Brush with a little beaten egg. Bake for about 15 minutes, until golden brown.

SERVES SIX

ANNA POTATOES

fat for greasing
1 kg / 2¼ lb even-sized potatoes
salt and pepper
melted clarified butter (Mrs Beeton's Tip, page 23)

Grease a 20-cm / 8-inch round cake tin and line the base with greased greaseproof paper. Set the oven at 190°C / 375°F / gas 5.

Trim the potatoes so that they will give equal-sized slices. Slice them very thinly using either a sharp knife or a mandoline. Arrange a layer of potatoes, slightly overlapping, in the base of the tin. Add salt and pepper to taste, then spoon a little clarified butter over them. Make a second layer of potatoes and spoon some more butter over them. Complete these layers until all the potatoes have been used. Cover the tin with greased greaseproof paper and foil.

Bake for 1 hour. Check the potatoes several times during cooking and add a little more clarified butter if they become too dry. Invert the tin on to a warm serving dish to remove the potatoes. Serve at once.

SERVES SIX

GRATIN DAUPHINOIS

25 g / 1 oz butter
1 kg / 2¼ lb, potatoes, thinly sliced
1 large onion, about 200 g / 7 oz, thinly sliced
200 g / 7 oz Gruyère cheese, grated
salt and pepper
grated nutmeg
125 ml / 4 fl oz single cream

Butter a 1.5-litre / 2¾-pint casserole, reserving the remaining butter. Set the oven at 190°C / 375°F / gas 5. Bring a saucepan of water to the boil, add the potatoes and onion, then blanch for 30 seconds. Drain.

Put a layer of potatoes in the bottom of the prepared casserole. Dot with a little of the butter, then sprinkle with some of the onion and cheese, a little salt, pepper and grated nutmeg. Pour over some of the cream. Repeat the layers until all the ingredients have been used, finishing with a layer of cheese. Pour the remaining cream on top.

Cover and bake for 1 hour. Remove from the oven and place under a hot grill for 5 minutes, until the top of the cheese is golden brown and bubbling.

SERVES SIX

SCALLOPED POTATOES WITH ONIONS

butter for greasing
675 g / 1½ lb potatoes, peeled and cut into 5-mm / ¼-inch slices
450 g / 1 lb onions, sliced in rings
salt and pepper
125 ml / 4 fl oz milk or cream
20 ml / 4 tsp butter

Grease a baking dish. Set the oven at 190°C / 375°F / gas 5. Layer the potatoes and onions in the prepared dish, sprinkling salt and pepper between the layers and ending with potatoes. Pour the milk or cream over the top. Dot the surface with butter and cover with foil or a lid.

Bake for 1½ hours, removing the cover for the last 20–30 minutes of the cooking time to allow the potatoes on the top to brown.

SERVES FOUR TO SIX

ROAST PARSNIPS

Look for firm, unblemished parsnips. Allow ½ large parsnip per person. To prepare them, peel, then cut them in half, in chunks or slices.

To roast parsnips arrange them around a joint of meat or in a separate dish and brush with fat. Allow about 45 minutes–1¼ hours at 180–190°C / 350–375°F / gas 4–5, until tender and golden.

Try drizzling the roasting parsnips with runny honey 10 minutes before the end of cooking time.

MRS BEETON'S TIP

Prepare the parsnips a day ahead and store in an airtight bag in the fridge until ready to use.

BRUSSELS SPROUTS

This winter vegetable is one of the traditional accompaniments to roast turkey. Look for small firm sprouts which are slightly shiny and green. Avoid very loose, yellowing or insect-nibbled sprouts.

Wash the sprouts thoroughly and remove any damaged leaves. Cut a cross in the stalk of larger ones so that they cook evenly. Add to a saucepan of boiling water and cook for 5–10 minutes.

BRUSSELS SPROUTS WITH CHESTNUTS

This is a classic accompaniment to the Christmas turkey. The slightly sweet flavour of the chestnuts is the perfect foil for the Brussels sprouts.

225 g / 8 oz chestnuts, shelled
(see Microwave Tip opposite and page 3)
1 kg / 2¼ lb Brussels sprouts
75 g / 3 oz cooked ham, finely chopped
60 ml / 4 tbsp single cream
salt and pepper

Set the oven at 180°C / 350°F / gas 4. Place the cleaned nuts in a saucepan, just cover with water and bring to the boil. Cover the pan, lower the heat, and simmer for about 20 minutes or until the nuts are tender. Drain, then cut each chestnut into quarters.

Trim the sprouts, pulling off any damaged leaves. Using a sharp knife, cut a cross in the base of each. Cook the sprouts in a saucepan of salted boiling water for 5–10 minutes until just tender. Drain well.

Combine the sprouts, chestnuts and ham in a small casserole. Stir in the cream and season with salt and pepper. Cover and bake for 15 minutes.

SERVES SIX

MICROWAVE TIP

Shelling chestnuts is made a lot easier by using the microwave. Make a slit in the shell of each nut, then rinse them thoroughly but do not dry them. Put the damp nuts in a bowl, cover loosely and cook on High for 5 minutes. When cool enough to handle, remove the shells.

GLAZED CARROTS

50 g / 2 oz butter
575 g / 1¼ lb young carrots, scraped but left whole
3 sugar cubes, crushed
1.25 ml / ¼ tsp salt
beef stock (see method)
15 ml / 1 tbsp chopped parsley to garnish

Melt the butter in a saucepan. Add the carrots, sugar and salt. Pour in enough stock to half cover the carrots. Cook over gentle heat, without covering the pan, for 15–20 minutes or until the carrots are tender. Shake the pan occasionally to prevent sticking.

Using a slotted spoon, transfer the carrots to a bowl and keep hot. Boil the stock rapidly in the pan until it is reduced to a rich glaze. Return the carrots to the pan, two or three at a time, turning them in the glaze until thoroughly coated. Place on a heated serving dish, garnish with parsley and serve at once.

SERVES SIX

CARROTS WITH CIDER

This traditional way of cooking carrots was originally known as the 'conservation method' because it preserved as many of the nutrients as possible.

75 g / 3 oz butter
675 g / 1½ lb young carrots, trimmed and scraped
salt
60 ml / 4 tbsp double cream
125 ml / 4 fl oz dry cider
few drops of lemon juice
pepper

Melt 25 g / 1 oz of the butter in a heavy-bottomed saucepan. Add the carrots and cook over very gentle heat for 10 minutes, shaking the pan frequently so that the carrots do not stick to the base. Pour over 100 ml / 3½ fl oz boiling water, with salt to taste. Cover the pan and simmer the carrots for about 10 minutes more or until tender. Drain, reserving the liquid for use in soup or stock.

Melt the remaining butter in the clean pan. Gradually stir in the cream and cider. Add the lemon juice and salt and pepper to taste. Stir in the carrots, cover the pan and cook gently for 10 minutes more. Serve at once.

SERVES SIX

MRS BEETON'S TIP

Another way of preserving as many nutrients as possible is to cook the carrots in the microwave, but the results will be more satisfactory if smaller quantities are used. Combine 225 g / 8 oz young carrots with 30 ml / 2 tbsp butter in a dish. Cover loosely and cook on High for 5–7 minutes, stirring once. Before serving, add salt and pepper to taste.

BUTTERED LEEKS

50 g / 2 oz butter
675 g / 1½ lb leeks, trimmed, sliced and washed
15 ml / 1 tbsp lemon juice
salt and pepper
30 ml / 2 tbsp single cream (optional)

Melt the butter in a heavy-bottomed saucepan. Add the leeks and lemon juice, with salt and pepper to taste. Cover the pan and cook the leeks over very gentle heat for about 30 minutes or until very tender. Shake the pan from time to time to prevent the leeks from sticking to the base. Serve in the cooking liquid. Stir in the cream when serving, if liked.

SERVES FOUR

MRS BEETON'S TIP

Leeks can be very gritty. The easiest way to wash them is to trim the roots and tough green leaves, slit them lengthways to the centre, and hold them open under cold running water to flush out the grit.

CAULIFLOWER CHEESE

salt and pepper
1 firm cauliflower
30 ml / 2 tbsp butter
60 ml / 4 tbsp plain flour
200 ml / 7 fl oz milk
125 g / 4½ oz Cheddar cheese, grated
pinch of dry mustard
pinch of cayenne pepper
25 g / 1 oz dried white breadcrumbs

Bring a saucepan of salted water to the boil, add the cauliflower, cover the pan and cook gently for 20–30 minutes until tender. Drain well, reserving 175 ml / 6 fl oz of the cooking water. Leave the cauliflower head whole or cut carefully into florets. Place in a warmed ovenproof dish, cover with greased greaseproof paper and keep hot.

Set the oven at 220°C / 425°F / gas 7, or preheat the grill. Melt the butter in a saucepan, stir in the flour and cook for 1 minute. Gradually add the milk and reserved cooking water, stirring all the time until the sauce boils and thickens. Remove from the heat and stir in 100 g / 4 oz of the cheese, stirring until it melts into the sauce. Add the mustard and cayenne and season with salt and pepper to taste.

Pour the sauce over the cauliflower. Mix the remaining cheese with the breadcrumbs and sprinkle them on top. Brown the topping for 7–10 minutes in the oven or under the grill. Serve at once.

SERVES FOUR

VARIATIONS

- A wide variety of vegetables can be cooked in this way. Try broccoli (particularly good with grilled bacon); small whole onions; celery, celeriac; leeks or chicory (both taste delicious if wrapped in ham before being covered in the cheese sauce) and asparagus. A mixed vegetable gratin – cooked sliced carrots, green beans, onions and potatoes – also works well. Vary the cheese topping too: Red Leicester has good flavour and colour; Gruyère or Emmental is tasty with leeks or chicory; a little blue cheese mixed with the Cheddar will enliven celery or celeriac.

CAULIFLOWER POLONAISE

1 large cauliflower, trimmed
salt
50 g / 2 oz butter
50 g / 2 oz fresh white breadcrumbs
2 hard-boiled eggs
15 ml / 1 tbsp chopped parsley

Put the cauliflower, stem down, in a saucepan. Pour over boiling water, add salt to taste and cook for 10–15 minutes or until the stalk is just tender. Drain the cauliflower thoroughly in a colander.

Meanwhile, melt the butter in a frying pan, add the breadcrumbs and fry until crisp and golden.

Chop the egg whites finely. Sieve the yolks and mix them with the parsley in a small bowl.

Drain the cauliflower thoroughly and place it on a heated serving dish. Sprinkle first with the breadcrumbs and then with the egg yolk mixture. Arrange the chopped egg white around the edge of the dish. Serve at once.

SERVES FOUR

PETITS POIS À LA FRANÇAISE

50 g / 2 oz butter
1 lettuce heart, shredded
1 bunch of spring onions, finely chopped
675 g / 1½ lb fresh shelled garden peas or frozen petits pois
pinch of sugar
salt and pepper

Melt the butter in a heavy-bottomed saucepan and add the lettuce, spring onions, peas and sugar, with salt and pepper to taste. Cover and simmer very gently until the peas are tender. Frozen petits pois may be ready in less than 10 minutes, but fresh garden peas could take 25 minutes.

SERVES SIX

COURGETTES WITH ALMONDS

The cooked courgettes should be firm and full flavoured, not overcooked and watery.

25 g / 1 oz butter
25 g / 1 oz blanched almonds, split in half
450 g / 1 lb courgettes, trimmed and thinly sliced
salt and pepper
30 ml / 2 tbsp snipped chives or chopped parsley

Melt the butter in a large frying pan. Add the almonds and fry over moderate heat, stirring, until lightly browned. Tip the courgettes into the pan and cook, regularly turning the slices until golden.

Tip the courgettes into a heated serving dish, add salt and pepper to taste and sprinkle the chives or parsley over them. Serve at once.

SERVES FOUR TO SIX

CELERIAC PURÉE

15 ml / 1 tbsp lemon juice
1 large celeriac root, about 1 kg / 2¼ lb
salt and white pepper
90 ml / 6 tbsp single cream
15 ml / 1 tbsp butter
60 ml / 4 tbsp pine nuts

Have ready a large saucepan of water to which the lemon juice has been added. Peel the celeriac root fairly thickly so that the creamy white flesh is exposed. Cut it into 1 cm / ½ inch cubes. Add the cubes to the acidulated water and bring to the boil over moderate heat. Add salt to taste, if desired, and cook for 8–10 minutes or until the celeriac is tender.

Drain the celeriac and purée it with the cream and butter in a blender or food processor. Alternatively, mash until smooth, then press through a sieve into a bowl. Reheat the purée if necessary, adjust the seasoning, stir in the nuts and serve at once.

SERVES FOUR

VARIATION

- **Celeriac and Potato Purée** Substitute potato for half the celeriac. Cook and purée as suggested above.

MICROWAVE TIP

The celeriac can be cooked in the microwave. Toss the celeriac cubes in acidulated water, drain off all but 60 ml / 4 tbsp, and put the mixture in a roasting bag. Close the bag lightly with an elastic band and cook on High for 15 minutes. Shake the bag once during cooking. It will be very hot, so protect your hand in an oven glove. Drain by snipping an end off the bag and holding it over the sink. Purée as above.

FENNEL WITH LEEKS

4 fennel bulbs, trimmed and halved
juice of ½ lemon
knob of butter or 30 ml / 2 tbsp olive oil
4 leeks, sliced
1 bay leaf
2 fresh thyme sprigs
salt and pepper
150 ml / ¼ pint chicken or vegetable stock
45 ml / 3 tbsp dry sherry (optional)

Set the oven at 180°C / 350°F / gas 4. As soon as the fennel is prepared, sprinkle the lemon juice over the cut bulbs. Heat the butter or oil in a frying pan and sauté the leeks for 2 minutes to soften them slightly. Add the pieces of fennel to the pan, pushing the leeks to one side. Turn the pieces of fennel in the fat for a minute or so, then tip the contents of the pan into an ovenproof casserole.

Add the bay leaf and thyme to the vegetables and season with salt and pepper to taste. Pour the stock and sherry (if used) over the fennel and cover the dish. Bake for 1–1¼ hours until tender, turning the vegetable mixture twice. Taste for seasoning, remove the bay leaf and serve.

SERVES FOUR

ITALIAN SPINACH

25 g / 1 oz sultanas
1 kg / 2¼ lb spinach
30 ml / 2 tbsp oil
1 garlic clove, crushed
salt and pepper
25 g / 1 oz pine nuts

Put the sultanas in a small bowl or mug, pour on boiling water to cover and set aside for 2–3 minutes until plumped. Drain well and set the sultanas aside.

Wash the fresh spinach several times and remove any coarse stalks. Put into a saucepan with just the water that clings to the leaves, then cover the pan. Put the pan over high heat for 2–3 minutes, shaking it frequently. Lower the heat, stir the spinach and cook for a further 5 minutes, turning the spinach occasionally, until cooked to your liking. Drain thoroughly, then chop the spinach coarsely.

Heat the oil in a large frying pan. Add the spinach and garlic, with salt and pepper to taste. Turn the spinach over and over in the pan with a wide spatula to heat it thoroughly without frying. Turn into a heated serving bowl, add the sultanas and nuts and mix lightly. Serve at once.

SERVES FOUR

PANFRIED ONION AND APPLE

40 g / 1½ oz butter
350 g / 12 oz onions, sliced in rings
450 g / 1 lb cooking apples
10 ml / 2 tsp caster sugar
salt and pepper

Melt the butter in a heavy-bottomed frying pan. Add the onions and fry gently. Peel, core and slice the apples into the pan. Mix lightly to coat the apples in the melted butter. Sprinkle the sugar over the top, cover and simmer for 30 minutes or until the onions and apples are tender. Season with salt and pepper to taste before serving.

SERVES FOUR

GLAZED ONIONS

Glazed onions make a tasty accompaniment to grilled steak, baked ham or bacon chops. They are often used as a garnish.

400 g / 14 oz button onions
Chicken Stock (page 18) (see method)
salt and pepper
15 ml / 1 tbsp soft light brown sugar
25 g / 1 oz butter
pinch of grated nutmeg

Skin the onions and put them in a single layer in a large saucepan. Add just enough stock to cover. Bring to a simmering point and cook for 15–20 minutes until the onions are just tender, adding a small amount of extra stock if necessary.

By the time the onions are cooked, the stock should have reduced almost to a glaze. Remove from the heat and stir in the remaining ingredients. Turn the onions over with a spoon so that the added ingredients mix well and the onions are coated in the mixture.

Return the pan to the heat until the onions become golden and glazed. Serve at once, with the remaining syrupy glaze.

SERVES FOUR

VARIATION

- **Citrus Glazed Onions** Melt 25 g / 1 oz butter in a frying pan. Add 400 g / 14 oz button onions. Sprinkle with 15 ml / 1 tbsp soft light brown sugar. Add salt and pepper to taste and fry, turning the onions occasionally until golden brown. Stir in 150 ml / ¼ pint orange juice and 10 ml / 2 tsp lemon juice. Cover and simmer for 15 minutes.

CREAMED ONIONS

butter for greasing
1 kg / 2¼ lb small onions, peeled but left whole
100 ml / 3½ fl oz double cream
Béchamel Sauce (page 154) made using 300 ml / ½ pint milk
grated nutmeg
salt and pepper
25 g / 1 oz butter
50 g / 2 oz dried white breadcrumbs
30 ml / 2 tbsp chopped parsley

Grease a 1-litre/ 1¾-pint casserole. Set the oven at 160°C / 325°F / gas 3. Bring a saucepan of water to the boil. Add the onions and cook for 10–15 minutes until just tender. Drain well.

Add the double cream to the Béchamel Sauce and reheat gently without boiling. Stir in the nutmeg with salt and pepper to taste, add the onions and mix lightly.

Spoon the mixture into the prepared casserole. Top with the breadcrumbs and dot with the butter. Bake for 20 minutes. Serve hot, sprinkled with the parsley.

SERVES SIX TO EIGHT

MRS BEETON'S TIP

To make about 100 g / 4 oz dried breadcrumbs, cut the crusts off six slices (175 g / 6 oz) of bread, then spread the bread out on baking sheets. Bake in a preheated 150°C / 300°F / gas 2 oven for about 30 minutes until dry but not browned. Cool, then crumb in a food processor or blender. Alternatively, put the dried bread between sheets of greaseproof paper and crush with a rolling pin.

MUSHROOMS IN CREAM SAUCE

50 g / 2 oz butter
450 g / 1 lb small button mushrooms
10 ml / 2 tsp arrowroot
125 ml / 4 fl oz Chicken Stock (page 18) or Vegetable Stock (page 20)
15 ml / 1 tbsp lemon juice
30 ml / 2 tbsp double cream
salt and pepper
30 ml / 2 tbsp chopped parsley

Melt the butter in large frying pan, add the mushrooms and fry over gentle heat without browning for 10 minutes.

Put the arrowroot in a small bowl. Stir in 30 ml / 2 tbsp of the stock until smooth. Add the remaining stock to the mushrooms and bring to the boil. Lower the heat and simmer gently for 15 minutes, stirring occasionally. Stir in the arrowroot, bring to the boil, stirring, then remove the pan from the heat.

Stir in the lemon juice and cream, with salt and pepper to taste. Serve sprinkled with parsley.

SERVES FOUR TO SIX

MUSHROOMS WITH BACON AND WINE

6 rindless streaky bacon rashers, chopped
400 g / 14 oz button mushrooms, halved or quartered if large
5 ml / 1 tsp snipped chives
5 ml / 1 tsp chopped parsley
10 ml / 2 tsp plain flour
75 ml / 5 tbsp white wine or cider
salt and pepper

Cook the bacon gently in a heavy-bottomed saucepan until the fat begins to run, then increase the heat to moderate and fry for 10 minutes. Add the mushrooms and herbs, tossing them in the bacon fat.

Sprinkle the flour over the mushrooms and cook for 1 minute, stirring gently. Add the wine or cider and simmer for 10 minutes, stirring occasionally. Season to taste and serve.

SERVES SIX

MRS BEETON'S TIP

Store mushrooms in a paper bag inside a polythene bag. The paper absorbs condensation and the mushrooms keep for three days in the refrigerator.

STUFFED MUSHROOMS

butter for greasing
12 large flat mushrooms
25 g / 1 oz butter or margarine
1 onion, finely chopped
50 g / 2 oz cooked ham (optional), finely chopped
15 ml / 1 tbsp fresh breadcrumbs
10 ml / 2 tsp grated Parmesan cheese
10 ml / 2 tsp chopped parsley
white wine
salt and pepper

Generously grease an ovenproof dish. Set the oven at 190°C / 375°F / gas 5.

Clean the mushrooms and remove the stalks. Place the caps in the prepared dish, gills uppermost. Chop the stalks finely. Melt the butter or margarine in a pan and fry the mushroom stalks and onion gently for 5 minutes. Add the ham to the onion mixture together with the breadcrumbs, Parmesan and parsley. Add just enough white wine to bind the mixture together. Add salt and pepper to taste.

Divide the stuffing mixture between the mushroom caps, heaping it up in the centre. Cover and bake for 25 minutes.

SERVES SIX

BRAISED CHESTNUTS WITH ONION AND CELERY

600 ml / 1 pint beef stock
1 kg / 2¼ lb chestnuts, peeled (see pages 3 and 111)
1 small onion stuck with 2 cloves
1 celery stick, roughly chopped
1 bay leaf
1 blade of mace
pinch of cayenne pepper
salt
puff pastry fleurons (see Mrs Beeton's Tip), to garnish

Bring the stock to the boil in a saucepan. Add the chestnuts, onion, celery, bay leaf, mace and cayenne, with a little salt. Cover and simmer for about 30 minutes, until the nuts are tender.

Drain the chestnuts, reserving the cooking liquid, and keep them hot in a serving dish. Chop the onion, discarding the cloves, and add it to the chestnuts. Discard the bay leaf and mace. Return the cooking liquid to the clean pan. Boil the liquid rapidly until it is reduced to a thin glaze. Pour the glaze over the chestnuts and garnish with the pastry fleurons.

SERVES SIX

MRS BEETON'S TIP

To make pastry fleurons, roll out 215 g / 7½ oz puff pastry on a floured board. Cut into rounds, using a 5-cm / 2-inch cutter. Move the cutter halfway across each round and cut in half again, making a half moon and an almond shape. Arrange the half moons on a baking sheet, brush with beaten egg and bake in a preheated 200°C / 400°F / gas 6 oven for 8–10 minutes. The almond shapes may either be baked as biscuits or re-rolled and cut to make more fleurons.

BAVARIAN CABBAGE

75 g / 3 oz butter
1 onion, finely chopped
1.1 kg / 2½ lb white cabbage, washed, quartered and shredded
1 cooking apple
salt and pepper
10 ml / 2 tsp sugar
125 ml / 4 fl oz Vegetable Stock (page 20) or water
1.25 ml / ¼ tsp caraway seeds
15 ml / 1 tbsp cornflour
60 ml / 4 tbsp white wine

Melt the butter in a heavy-bottomed saucepan. Add the onion and fry gently for 10 minutes until soft but not coloured. Stir in the cabbage, tossing it lightly in the fat.

Peel and core the apple, chop it finely and stir it into the pan. Add salt and pepper to taste, then stir in the sugar, stock or water, and caraway seeds. Cover the pan with a tight-fitting lid and simmer very gently for 1 hour.

Meanwhile mix the comflour and wine together in a small bowl. Stir the mixture into the pan. Bring to the boil, stirring the mixture constantly until it thickens. Cook for 2–3 minutes, still stirring. Serve at once.

SERVES SIX

VARIATION

For a slightly more fruity flavour, use two apples and substitute cider for the stock and wine. Omit the caraway seeds.

SAUERKRAUT WITH JUNIPER BERRIES

One of the oldest forms of preserved food, sauerkraut is simply fermented cabbage. It is sometimes possible to buy it loose from a large barrel in a delicatessen, but is more generally sold in cans or jars.

400 g / 14 oz sauerkraut
50 g / 2 oz butter
4 rindless streaky bacon rashers, chopped
1 large onion, chopped
1 garlic clove, crushed
6 juniper berries, crushed
2 bay leaves
5 ml / 1 tsp caraway seeds
250 ml / 9 fl oz Chicken Stock (page 18)
salt and pepper (optional)

Put the sauerkraut in a large bowl, pour in enough cold water to cover and soak for 15 minutes. Drain thoroughly, then squeeze dry.

Melt the butter in a saucepan, add the bacon and onion and fry over gentle heat for about 10 minutes. Add all the remaining ingredients, cover the pan and simmer for 1 hour. Add salt and pepper, if required, before serving.

SERVES FOUR

MRS BEETON'S TIP

For a richer, creamier flavour, stir in 150 ml / ¼ pint plain yogurt or soured cream just before serving the sauerkraut. Do not allow the mixture to approach boiling point after adding the yogurt or cream.

PEASE PUDDING

575 g / 1¼ lb split peas, soaked overnight in cold water to cover
1 small onion, peeled but left whole
1 bouquet garni
salt and pepper
50 g / 2 oz butter, cut into small pieces
2 eggs, beaten

Drain the peas, put them in a saucepan and add cold water to cover. Add the onion, the bouquet garni and salt and pepper to taste. Bring to the boil, skim off any scum on the surface of the liquid, then reduce the heat to very low and simmer the peas for 2–2½ hours or until tender.

Drain the peas thoroughly. Press them through a sieve or purée in a blender or food processor. Add the pieces of butter with the beaten eggs. Beat well.

Spoon the mixture into a floured pudding cloth and tie tightly. Suspend the bag in a large saucepan of boiling salted water and simmer gently for 1 hour. Remove from the pan, take the pudding out of the cloth and serve very hot.

SERVES SIX

MRS BEETON'S TIP

Modern cooks, unfamiliar with pudding cloths, can bake this nutritious pudding in a greased casserole. It will need about 30 minutes to cook in a preheated 180°C / 350°F / gas 4 oven.

Stuffings

Stuffings are very easy to make, surprisingly versatile and delicious. Not only for poultry, meat and fish, they can also be used to stuff vegetables, as coatings and toppings, and in meatballs and burgers.

STUFFINGS

The simplest stuffing combination to store or freeze consists of breadcrumbs with parsley and thyme. Unless both herbs and crumbs are thoroughly dried, they should be frozen. Add milk or egg to bind, if necessary, when thawed. When freezing any stuffing always include a detailed label. Although you may be convinced you will remember how the aromatic lemon and raisin stuffing was made, three months later you will probably have difficulty in deciding whether or not it is appropriate for fish.

The best types of stuffings to freeze in large quantities are the ones that go well with everything. Consider these combinations:

- Breadcrumbs or cooked rice with lemon rind, chopped parsley, raisins and lightly cooked diced onion. Good with cod steaks, chicken, duck, pork chops or lamb.
- Wholemeal breadcrumbs with marjoram, peeled and chopped tomato, and par-cooked finely chopped onion. Open freeze the mixture to prevent it from forming a lump, then break it up and pack. Use with pork, lamb or in beef olives (rolled slices of meat). The stuffing may also be mixed with minced beef, lamb or pork to make meat loaf, burgers or meatballs.
- Lightly cooked finely chopped onion and garlic mixed with grated fresh root ginger and a little chopped green chilli makes a good flavouring. Mix with breadcrumbs, a sprinkling of ground coriander and a little chopped fresh coriander to create an excellent spicy stuffing for chicken breasts or lamb breast. Mixed with minced lamb, it makes delicious meatballs.
- Breadcrumbs or cooked lentils, grated orange rind, thyme or rosemary, parsley and cooked finely chopped onion is another winning mixture. Open freeze, then pack in chunks. Use with pork, lamb, duck or vegetables. Add some finely chopped nuts and use to make vegetarian burgers.
- Mixed with grated cheese, breadcrumb stuffing mixes make excellent gratin toppings or toppings for savoury crumble.
- Use breadcrumb mixes to coat chicken breasts, then bake in the oven until cooked and golden.

CHESTNUT STUFFING

800 g / 1¾ lb chestnuts, shelled (see pages 3 and 111)
150–250 ml / 5–9 fl oz Chicken Stock (page 18) or Vegetable Stock (page 20)
50 g / 2 oz butter, softened
pinch of ground cinnamon
2.5 ml / ½ tsp sugar
salt and pepper

Put the shelled chestnuts in a saucepan and add the stock. Bring to the boil, lower the heat, cover and simmer until the chestnuts are tender. Drain, reserving the stock.

Rub the chestnuts through a fine wire sieve into a bowl. Add the butter, cinnamon and sugar, with salt and pepper to taste. Stir in enough of the reserved stock to bind.

SUFFICIENT FOR THE NECK END OF 1 x 5–6 kg / 11–13 lb TURKEY; USE HALF THE QUANTITY FOR 1 x 1.5 kg / 3¼ lb CHICKEN

MRS BEETON'S TIP

Canned chestnuts may be used for the stuffing. You will require about 450 g / 1 lb.

CHESTNUT AND ONION STUFFING

Use double the quantity listed below when stuffing the neck end of a 5–6 kg / 11–13 lb turkey.

1 large onion, thickly sliced
125 ml / 4 fl oz Chicken Stock (page 18) or water
450 g / 1 lb chestnuts, prepared and cooked (see Mrs Beeton's Tip)
or 300 g / 11 oz canned chestnuts
salt and pepper
1 egg, beaten

Combine the onion and stock or water in a small saucepan. Bring the liquid to the boil, lower the heat and simmer for about 10 minutes until the onion is tender, drain and chop finely.

Meanwhile mince the chestnuts or chop them finely. Combine the chestnuts and onion in a bowl, stir in salt and pepper to taste and add enough of the egg to bind the stuffing.

SUFFICIENT FOR 1 x 2.5 kg / 5½ lb DUCK

MRS BEETON'S TIP

To prepare chestnuts, make a slit in the rounded side of each nut, then bake them in a preheated 180°C / 350°F / gas 4 oven for 30 minutes or cook them in boiling water for 20 minutes. Remove the shells and skins while still hot. Put the shelled nuts in a saucepan with just enough stock to cover. Bring the liquid to the boil, lower the heat and simmer for 45–60 minutes or until the nuts are tender.

APPLE AND CELERY STUFFING

3 rindless streaky bacon rashers, chopped
1 onion, finely chopped
1 celery stick, finely sliced
3 large cooking apples
75 g / 3 oz fresh white breadcrumbs
15 ml / 1 tbsp grated lemon rind
salt and pepper

Heat the bacon gently in a frying pan until the fat runs, then increase the heat and fry until browned, stirring frequently. Using a slotted spoon, transfer the bacon to a bowl. Add the onion and celery to the fat remaining in the frying pan and fry over moderate heat for 5 minutes. Remove with a slotted spoon, add to the bacon and mix lightly.

Peel, core and dice the apples. Add them to the pan and fry until soft and lightly browned. Add to the bacon mixture with the breadcrumbs and lemon rind. Mix well, adding salt and pepper to taste.

SUFFICIENT FOR 1 x 4–5 kg / 9–11 lb GOOSE, 2 x 2.5 kg / 5½ lb DUCKS OR 1 BONED PORK JOINT

MRS BEETON'S TIP

Many delicatessens and deli counters in supermarkets sell packets of bacon bits – the trimmings left after slicing. These are ideal for a recipe such as this, and may also be used in quiches, on pizzas and to flavour soups and stews.

HERB STUFFING

Keeping a stock of stuffing in the freezer means that chicken, fish fillets and boned joints can be prepared swiftly for the oven. Use double the quantity below to stuff the neck end of a 5–6 kg / 11–13 lb turkey.

50 g / 2 oz butter or margarine
100 g / 4 oz soft white or granary breadcrumbs
pinch of grated nutmeg
15 ml / 1 tbsp chopped parsley
5 ml / 1 tsp chopped fresh mixed herbs
grated rind of ½ lemon
salt and pepper
1 egg, beaten

Melt the butter or margarine in a small saucepan and stir in the breadcrumbs, nutmeg, herbs and lemon rind. Add salt and pepper to taste. Stir in enough of the beaten egg to bind the mixture.

SUFFICIENT FOR 1 x 1.5–2 kg / 3¼–4½ lb CHICKEN, A BONED JOINT OF VEAL OR 8 x 75 g / 3 oz FISH FILLETS

MRS BEETON'S TIP

A bird, joint of meat or fish should always be stuffed just before being cooked. If preferred, the stuffing may be shaped into 12 or 16 small balls and baked in a preheated 180°C / 350°F / gas 4 oven for 15–20 minutes.

LEMON AND HERB STUFFING

50 g / 2 oz butter
100 g / 4 oz fresh white breadcrumbs
30 ml / 2 tbsp chopped parsley
2.5 ml / ½ tsp chopped fresh thyme
grated rind of ½ lemon
salt and pepper

Melt the butter in a small saucepan. Add the breadcrumbs, herbs and lemon rind. Add salt and pepper to taste, then use as required.

SUFFICIENT FOR 8 x 75 g / 3 oz THIN FISH FILLETS

WALNUT STUFFING

15 g / ½ oz butter
1 small onion, finely chopped
12 whole walnuts or 24 halves, chopped
50 g / 2 oz sausagemeat
50 g / 2 oz fresh white breadcrumbs
2.5 ml / ½ tsp dried mixed herbs
1 large cooking apple
salt and pepper
1 egg, lightly beaten
milk (see method)

Melt the butter in a saucepan, add the onion and cook over very gentle heat for about 10 minutes until soft and pale golden. Combine the walnuts, sausagemeat, breadcrumbs and herbs in a bowl. Peel, core and chop the apple. Add it to the bowl, with salt and pepper to taste. Stir in the onion with the melted butter and mix well. Bind with the egg, adding a little milk if necessary.

SUFFICIENT FOR 1 x 2.5 kg / 5½ lb DUCK; DOUBLE THE QUANTITY FOR 1 x 4–5 kg / 8–11 lb GOOSE

SAGE AND ONION STUFFING

2 onions, thickly sliced
4 young fresh sage sprigs or
10 ml / 2 tsp dried sage
100 g / 4 oz fresh white breadcrumbs
50 g / 2 oz butter or margarine, melted
salt and pepper
1 egg, lightly beaten (optional)

Put the onions in a small saucepan with water to cover. Bring to the boil, cook for 2–3 minutes, then remove the onions from the pan with a slotted spoon. Chop them finely. Chop the sage leaves finely, discarding any stalk.

Combine the breadcrumbs, onions and sage in a bowl. Add the melted butter or margarine and season with salt and pepper to taste. Mix well. If the stuffing is to be shaped into balls, bind it with the beaten egg.

SUFFICIENT FOR 1 x 2.5 kg / 5½ lb DUCK;
DOUBLE THE QUANTITY FOR 1 x 4–5 kg / 9–11 lb GOOSE

WILD RICE STUFFING

This stuffing is particularly recommended for game birds.

350 ml / 12 fl oz stock
150 g / 5 oz wild rice
50 g / 2 oz butter
2 shallots, finely chopped
½ small green pepper, finely chopped
1 small celery stick, finely sliced
100 g / 4 oz mushrooms, chopped
30 ml / 2 tbsp tomato purée

Bring the stock to the boil in a saucepan and add the wild rice. Lower the heat, cover and cook gently for 40 minutes until the rice is almost tender and the majority of the stock is absorbed. Cover and set aside.

Melt the butter in a saucepan, add the shallots, green pepper, celery and mushrooms and fry over gentle heat for 3 minutes. Remove from the heat, add to the wild rice with the tomato purée and mix well.

SUFFICIENT FOR 2 PHEASANTS OR 1 LARGE GUINEAFOWL

APRICOT STUFFING

This stuffing is particularly good with pork, but may also be used with lamb, any poultry or game birds. Use double the quantity listed below when stuffing 1 x 4–5 kg / 9–11 lb goose.

75 g / 3 oz dried apricots, soaked overnight in water to cover
75 g / 3 oz soft white or granary breadcrumbs
25 g / 1 oz butter, melted
1.25 ml / ¼ tsp salt
1.25 ml / ¼ tsp freshly ground black pepper
pinch each of dried thyme, ground mace and grated nutmeg
1 celery stick, finely chopped

Drain the apricots, reserving the liquid, and chop finely. Put in a bowl with the breadcrumbs, butter, salt, pepper, thyme and spices. Stir in the celery and moisten the mixture with a little of the reserved apricot liquid.

SUFFICIENT FOR A BONED JOINT OF PORK OR 1 x 2.5 kg / 5½ lb DUCK

MRS BEETON'S TIP

Ready-to-eat dried apricots may be used for this stuffing, in which case the mixture should be moistened with a little vegetable or chicken stock.

PRUNE AND APPLE STUFFING

Use double the quantity listed below when stuffing a 4–5 kg / 9–11 lb goose.

100 g / 4 oz prunes, soaked overnight and drained
(see Mrs Beeton's Tip, opposite)
1 large cooking apple
100 g / 4 oz boiled long-grain white or brown rice
50 g / 2 oz flaked almonds
50 g / 2 oz butter, softened
salt and pepper
grated rind and juice of ½ lemon
1 egg, beaten

Stone and chop the prunes. Peel, core and roughly chop the apple. Combine the fruit in a bowl with the rice, almonds and butter. Add salt and pepper to taste and stir in the lemon rind and juice. Add enough beaten egg to moisten.

SUFFICIENT FOR A BONED JOINT OF PORK
OR 1 x 2.5 kg / 5½ lb DUCK

SAUSAGEMEAT STUFFING

1 chicken or turkey liver, trimmed (optional)
450 g / 1 lb pork sausagemeat
50 g / 2 oz fresh white breadcrumbs
15 ml / 1 tbsp chopped parsley
5 ml / 1 tsp dried mixed herbs
1 egg, lightly beaten
salt and pepper

If using the liver, chop it finely and put it in a mixing bowl. Add the sausagemeat and breadcrumbs, with the herbs. Stir in enough of the beaten egg to bind the mixture. Add plenty of salt and pepper.

SUFFICIENT FOR 1 x 1.5 kg / 3¼ lb CHICKEN;
TREBLE THE QUANTITY FOR 1 x 5–6 kg / 9–11 lb TURKEY

MRS BEETON'S TIP

Canned prunes may be used for the Prune and Apple Stuffing. Choose the variety canned in natural juice and substitute a little of the juice for half the lemon juice in the recipe.

MRS BEETON'S FORCEMEAT

100 g / 4 oz gammon or rindless bacon, finely chopped
50 g / 2 oz shredded beef suet
grated rind of 1 lemon
5 ml / 1 tsp chopped parsley
5 ml / 1 tsp chopped mixed herbs
salt and cayenne pepper
pinch of ground mace
150 g / 5 oz fresh white breadcrumbs
2 eggs, lightly beaten

Combine the gammon or bacon, suet, lemon rind and herbs in a bowl. Add salt, cayenne and mace to taste, mix well with a fork, then stir in the breadcrumbs. Gradually add enough beaten egg to bind.

MAKES ABOUT 350 g / 12 oz

VARIATION

- **Mrs Beeton's Forcemeat Balls** Roll the mixture into 6–8 small balls. Either cook the forcemeat balls around a roast joint or bird, or fry them in a little oil until browned and cooked through.

MUSHROOM STUFFING

Although this stuffing is recommended for fish, it is also very good with all poultry and game birds.

1 rindless streaky bacon rasher, chopped
100 g / 4 oz button mushrooms with stalks, chopped
100 g / 4 oz fresh white breadcrumbs
knob of butter or margarine
pinch of grated nutmeg
salt and pepper
1 egg

Put the bacon in a heavy-bottomed saucepan over moderate heat for about 2 minutes or until the fat runs.

Add the mushrooms and fry very gently for 3–5 minutes, stirring frequently. When the mushrooms soften, remove the pan from the heat and stir in the breadcrumbs, butter or margarine and nutmeg. Add salt and pepper to taste.

Beat the egg in a cup until it is just liquid, then stir enough of the beaten egg into the stuffing to bind it. Use as required.

SUFFICIENT FOR 8 x 75 g / 3 oz THIN FISH FILLETS

MRS BEETON'S TIP

It is a good idea to keep a stock of breadcrumbs in a sealed polythene bag in the freezer. They thaw swiftly and can be used in a wide variety of sweet and savoury dishes.

Savoury Sauces

Gravy, Cranberry Sauce and Bread Sauce are the essential British Christmas accompaniments. A variety of other straightforward and delicious sauces can transform simple ingredients into impressive meals.

GRAVY

giblets, carcass bones or trimmings from meat, poultry or game
1 bay leaf
1 thyme sprig
1 clove
6 black peppercorns
1 onion, sliced
pan juices from roasting (see Mrs Beeton's Tip)
25 g / 1 oz plain flour (optional)
salt and pepper

Place the giblets, bones, carcass and/or trimmings (for example wing ends) in a saucepan. Pour in water to cover, then add the bay leaf, thyme, clove, peppercorns and onion. Bring to the boil and skim off any scum, then lower the heat, cover the pan and simmer for about 1 hour.

Strain the stock and measure it. You need about 600–750 ml / 1–1¼ pints to make gravy for up to six servings. If necessary, pour the stock back into the saucepan and boil until reduced.

Pour off most of the fat from the roasting tin, leaving a thin layer and all the cooking juices. Place the tin over moderate heat; add the flour if the gravy is to be thickened. Cook the flour, stirring all the time and scraping all the sediment off the tin, for about 3 minutes, until it is browned. If the gravy is not thickened, pour in about 300 ml / ½ pint of the stock and boil, stirring and scraping, until the sediment on the base of the tin is incorporated.

Slowly pour in the stock (or the remaining stock, if making thin gravy), stirring all the time. Bring to the boil and cook for 2–3 minutes to reduce the gravy and concentrate the flavour slightly. Taste and add more salt and pepper if required.

SERVES FOUR TO SIX

MRS BEETON'S TIP

The quality of the sediment on the base of the cooking tin determines the quality of the gravy. If the meat was well seasoned and roasted until well browned outside, the sediment should have a good colour and flavour. Any herbs (other than large stalks), onions or flavouring roasted under the meat should be left in the pan until the gravy is boiled, then strained out before serving.

GRAVY NOTES

- If making gravy for a meal other than a roast, for example to accompany sausages or toad-in-the-hole, use a little fat instead of the pan juices and brown the flour well over low to moderate heat. Meat dripping gives the best flavour but butter or other fat may be used.
- To make onion gravy, slowly brown 2 thinly sliced onions in the fat before adding the flour – this is excellent with grilled sausages or toad-in-the-hole.
- Gravy browning may be added if necessary; however, it can make the sauce look artificial and unpleasant. Pale gravy is perfectly acceptable, provided it has good flavour.
- Always taste gravy when cooked. It should be well seasoned. If it lacks flavour, or is rather dull, a dash of Worcestershire sauce, mushroom ketchup or about 5–15 ml / 1–3 tsp tomato purée may be whisked in.
- Gravy may be enriched by adding up to half wine instead of stock.
- Add 60 ml / 4 tbsp port or sherry, and 15 ml / 1 tbsp redcurrant jelly to make a rich gravy for duck, game, lamb, pork or venison.
- Add 2 chopped pickled walnuts and 15 ml / 1 tbsp walnut oil to the pan juices to make a delicious walnut gravy.
- Use vegetable stock to make vegetable gravy. Cook a finely diced carrot and 2 thinly sliced onions in butter or margarine instead of using meat juices. Add 1.25 ml / ¼ tsp ground mace and 30 ml / 2 tbsp chopped parsley.
- Add 100 g / 4 oz thinly sliced mushrooms to the pan juices to make a mushroom gravy. The sauce may be further enriched by adding a little mushroom ketchup.

BREAD SAUCE

600 ml / 1 pint milk
1 large onion studded with 6 cloves
1 blade of mace
4 peppercorns
1 allspice berry
1 bay leaf
100 g / 4 oz fine fresh white breadcrumbs
15 ml / 1 tbsp butter
salt and pepper
freshly grated nutmeg
30 ml / 2 tbsp single cream (optional)

Put the milk in a small saucepan with the studded onion, mace, peppercorns, allspice and bay leaf. Bring very slowly to boiling point, then remove from the heat, cover the pan and set it aside for 30 minutes.

Strain the flavoured milk into a heatproof bowl, pressing the onion against the sides of the strainer to extract as much of the liquid as possible. Stir in the breadcrumbs and butter, with salt, pepper and nutmeg to taste.

Set the bowl over simmering water and cook for 20 minutes, stirring occasionally until thick and creamy. Stir in the cream, if using, just before serving.

MAKES ABOUT 250 ml / 9 fl oz

MICROWAVE TIP

There is no need to infuse the onion in the milk if the sauce is to be made in the microwave. Simply put the clove-studded onion in a deep bowl, cover and cook on High for 2 minutes. Add the spices, bay leaf and milk, cover loosely and cook on High for 6–6½ minutes. Stir in the remaining ingredients, except the cream, and cook for 2 minutes more. Remove the studded onion, whole spices and bay leaf. Whisk the sauce, adding the cream if liked.

CHESTNUT SAUCE

Serve this creamy sauce instead of chestnut stuffing with turkey. It also goes well with roast, grilled or pan-fried chicken.

225 g / 8 oz chestnuts
300 ml / ½ pint Chicken Stock (page 18)
2 strips of lemon rind
salt and pepper
cayenne pepper
150 ml / ¼ pint single cream
lemon juice

Make a small slit in the shell of each chestnut. Place the chestnuts in a saucepan of boiling water and cook for 15 minutes. Drain, carefully removing the shells and skins while the chestnuts are still very hot.

Put the peeled chestnuts in a pan and add the stock and lemon rind. Bring to the boil, lower the heat and simmer for 15 minutes.

Purée the chestnuts with the stock in a blender or food processor, or press through a fine sieve into a clean pan. Add salt, pepper and cayenne to taste. Stir in the cream and heat through without boiling. Add lemon juice to taste to sharpen the sauce. Serve at once.

SERVES SIX
(MAKES ABOUT 600 ml / 1 pint)

CRANBERRY SAUCE

150 g / 5 oz sugar
225 g / 8 oz cranberries

Put the sugar in a heavy-bottomed saucepan. Add 125 ml / 4 fl oz water. Stir over gentle heat until the sugar dissolves. Add the cranberries and cook gently for about 10 minutes until they have burst and are quite tender. Leave to cool.

MAKES ABOUT 300 ml / ½ pint

VARIATIONS

- **Cranberry and Apple** Use half cranberries and half tart cooking apples.
- **Cranberry and Orange** Use orange juice instead of water. Add 10 ml / 2 tsp finely grated orange rind.
- **Cranberry and Sherry** Add 30–45 ml / 2–3 tbsp sherry to the cranberries.

CRANBERRY AND APPLE JELLY

1 kg / 2¼ lb apples
700 g / 1½ lb cranberries
granulated sugar (see method)

Slice the apples without peeling or coring, and put in a pan with the cranberries and enough water to cover. Simmer gently until thoroughly mashed. Strain through a scalded jelly bag. Leave to drip for 1 hour.

Measure the extract, return it to the cleaned pan and heat gently. Add the required quantity of sugar (usually about 800 g / 1¾ lb for each litre / 1¾ pints of extract). Stir over a low heat until dissolved, the boil steadily until the setting point is reached. To test for this, spoon a little of the syrup onto a cold saucer. Leave to cool, then push a finger over the surface, which should wrinkle. Remove the jelly from the heat and skim. Pot in warm, sterilised jars, cover and label. Store in a cool, dry place.

MAKES ABOUT 1.75 litres / 3 pints

CUMBERLAND SAUCE

A rich, zesty sauce that may be served hot or cold with plain roast or grilled game.

grated rind and juice of 1 orange
grated rind and juice of 1 lemon
75 ml / 5 tbsp port
30 ml / 2 tbsp red wine vinegar
100 g / 4 oz redcurrant jelly
1.25 ml / ¼ tsp prepared mustard
salt and cayenne pepper

Combine the orange and lemon rind in a small saucepan. Add 75 ml / 5 tbsp water and heat to simmering point. Simmer gently for 10 minutes. Add the port, vinegar, redcurrant jelly and mustard, stirring until the jelly melts. Stir in the citrus juices and add salt and cayenne to taste. Simmer for 3–4 minutes, pour into a sauceboat and serve.

MAKES ABOUT 250 ml / 9 fl oz

MAÎTRE D'HÔTEL BUTTER

100 g / 4 oz butter
4–5 large parsley sprigs, finely chopped
salt and pepper
2.5 ml / ½ tsp lemon juice

Beat the butter until creamy in a small bowl. Add the parsley, a little at a time, beating until well combined. Add salt to taste and a small pinch of pepper. Add a few drops of lemon juice to intensify the flavour. Use at once or press into small pots, tapping the pots while filling to knock out all the air. Cover with foil and refrigerate until required. Use within two days.

MAKES 100 g / 4 oz

APPLE SAUCE

450 g / 1 lb apples
4 cloves
15 g / ½ oz butter
rind and juice of ½ lemon
sugar (see method)

Peel, core and slice the apples. Put them in a saucepan with 30 ml / 2 tbsp water, add the cloves, butter and lemon rind. Cover and cook over low heat until the apple is reduced to a pulp. Remove the cloves. Beat until smooth, rub through a sieve or process in a blender or food processor. Return the sauce to the clean pan, stir in the lemon juice and add sugar to taste. Reheat gently, stirring until the sugar has dissolved. Serve hot or cold.

MAKES ABOUT 350 ml / 12 fl oz

BROWN APPLE SAUCE

In Mrs Beeton's day, this tangy, apple-flavoured gravy was frequently served as an accompaniment to roast pork or goose. It is also suitable for grilled pork chops or gammon steaks.

350 g / 12 oz Bramley apples
300 ml / ½ pint Gravy (page 142), made with poultry or pork cooking juices
45 ml / 3 tbsp sugar
salt and pepper
cayenne pepper

Quarter, peel, core and slice the apples. Put them in a saucepan with the gravy. Bring to the boil, reduce the heat and cover the pan. Simmer for 10–15 minutes until the apple is reduced to a pulp. Beat the pulp into the gravy until smooth. Add the sugar with salt, pepper and cayenne to taste. Serve hot.

MAKES ABOUT 600 ml / 1 pint

PRUNE SAUCE

Prune sauce is rich and dark. Its sweet taste complements meats which are traditionally fatty, such as lamb or pork, and it also marries very well with venison. The prunes may be soaked in red wine or a mixture of half-and-half wine and water.

225 g / 8 oz prunes, soaked overnight in water to cover
strip of lemon rind
25 g / 1 oz sugar
pinch of ground cinnamon
15 ml / 1 tbsp rum or brandy (optional)
lemon juice

Transfer the prunes, with the soaking water, to a saucepan. Add the lemon rind and simmer for 10–15 minutes until tender. Strain the prunes, reserving the liquid. Remove the stones and discard the lemon rind.

Purée the prunes with the reserved liquid in a food processor or blender. Alternatively, rub the mixture through a sieve into a clean saucepan. Stir in the sugar and cinnamon. Reheat gently, stirring until all the sugar has dissolved. Stir in the rum or brandy (if using) and add lemon juice to taste. Serve at once, in a sauceboat.

MAKES ABOUT 350 ml / 12 fl oz

CHRISTOPHER NORTH'S SAUCE

Serve this potent sauce as a relish with roast beef, veal or game, or use it to pep up gravies and other sauces.

175 ml / 6 fl oz port
30 ml / 2 tbsp Worcestershire sauce
10 ml / 2 tsp mushroom ketchup
10 ml / 2 tsp caster sugar
15 ml / 1 tbsp lemon juice
1.25 ml / ¼ tsp cayenne pepper
2.5 ml / ½ tsp salt

Mix all the ingredients together in the top of a double saucepan or a heatproof bowl set over simmering water. Heat gently, without boiling. Serve at once or cool quickly and refrigerate in a closed jar until required.

MAKES ABOUT 250 ml / 9 fl oz

HORSERADISH SAUCE

60 ml / 4 tbsp grated horseradish
5 ml / 1 tsp caster sugar
5 ml / 1 tsp salt
2.5 ml / ½ tsp pepper
10 ml / 2 tsp prepared mustard
malt vinegar (see method)
45–60 ml / 3–4 tbsp single cream (optional)

Mix the horseradish, sugar, salt, pepper and mustard in a non- metallic bowl. Stir in enough vinegar to make a sauce with the consistency of cream. The flavour and appearance will be improved if the quantity of vinegar is reduced, and the single cream added.

MAKES ABOUT 150 ml / ¼ pint

TOMATO SAUCE

Tomato sauce has a multitude of uses in savoury cookery. It is one of the simplest accompaniments for plain cooked pasta, it is included in many baked dishes and it is, of course, excellent with grilled fish, poultry and meat.

30 ml / 2 tbsp olive oil
1 onion, finely chopped
1 garlic clove, crushed
1 bay leaf
1 rindless streaky bacon rasher, chopped (optional)
800 g / 1¾ lb canned tomatoes, peeled and chopped
60 ml / 4 tbsp stock or red wine
salt and pepper
generous pinch of sugar
15 ml / 1 tbsp chopped fresh basil or 5 ml / 1 tsp dried basil

Heat the oil in a saucepan and fry the onion, garlic, bay leaf and bacon, if using, over gentle heat for 15 minutes.

Stir in the remaining ingredients except the basil. Heat until bubbling, then cover the pan and simmer gently for 30 minutes or until the tomatoes are reduced to a pulp.

Rub the sauce through a sieve into a clean saucepan or purée in a blender or food processor until smooth, then rub it through a sieve to remove seeds, if required. Reheat the sauce. Add the basil. Add more salt and pepper if required before serving.

MAKES ABOUT 600 ml / 1 pint

HOLLANDAISE SAUCE

This is the classic sauce to serve with asparagus, poached salmon or other firm fish.

45 ml / 3 tbsp white wine vinegar
6 peppercorns
bay leaf
1 blade of mace
3 egg yolks
100 g / 4 oz butter, softened
salt and pepper

Combine the vinegar, peppercorns, bay leaf and mace in a small saucepan. Boil rapidly until the liquid is reduced to 15 ml / 1 tbsp. Strain into a heatproof bowl and leave to cool.

Add the egg yolks and a nut of butter to the vinegar and place over a pan of gently simmering water. Heat the mixture gently, beating constantly until thick. Do not allow it to approach boiling point.

Add the remaining butter, a little at a time, beating well after each addition. When all the butter has been added the sauce should be thick and glossy.

MICROWAVE TIP

A quick and easy Hollandaise Sauce can be made in the microwave oven. Combine 30 ml / 2 tbsp lemon juice with 15 ml / 1 tbsp water in a large bowl. Add a little salt and white pepper and cook on High for 3–6 minutes or until the mixture is reduced by about two-thirds. Meanwhile place 100 g / 4 oz butter in a measuring jug. Remove the bowl of lemon juice from the microwave oven, replacing it with the jug of butter. Heat the butter on High for 2½ minutes. Meanwhile add 2 large egg yolks to the lemon juice, whisking constantly. When the butter is hot, add it in the same way. Return the sauce to the microwave oven. Cook on High for 30 seconds, whisk once more and serve.

If the sauce curdles, whisk in 10 ml / 2 tsp cold water. If this fails to bind it, put an egg yolk in a clean bowl and beat in the sauce gradually. Add a little salt and pepper and serve the sauce lukewarm.

MAKES ABOUT 125 ml / 4 fl oz

BÉARNAISE SAUCE

The classic accompaniment to grilled beef steak, Béarnaise Sauce is also delicious with vegetables such as broccoli.

60 ml / 4 tbsp white wine vinegar
15 ml / 1 tbsp chopped shallot
5 black peppercorns, lightly crushed
1 bay leaf
2 fresh tarragon stalks, chopped, or
1.25 ml / ¼ tsp dried tarragon
1.25 ml / ¼ tsp dried thyme
2 egg yolks
100 g / 4 oz butter, cut into small pieces
salt and pepper

Combine the vinegar, chopped shallot, peppercorns and herbs in a small saucepan. Boil until the liquid is reduced to 15 ml / 1 tbsp, then strain into a heatproof bowl. Cool, then stir in the egg yolks.

Place the bowl over a saucepan of simmering water and whisk until the eggs start to thicken. Gradually add the butter, whisking after each addition, until the sauce is thick and creamy. Add salt and pepper to taste.

MAKES ABOUT 175 ml / 6 fl oz

BÉCHAMEL SAUCE

Marquis Louis de Béchameil is credited with inventing this French foundation sauce. For a slightly less rich version, use half white stock and half milk.

1 small onion, thickly sliced
1 small carrot, sliced
1 small celery stick, sliced
600 ml / 1 pint milk
1 bay leaf
few parsley stalks
1 fresh thyme sprig
1 clove
6 white peppercorns
1 blade of mace
salt
50 g / 2 oz butter
50 g / 2 oz plain flour
60 ml / 4 tbsp single cream (optional)

Combine the onion, carrot, celery and milk in a saucepan. Add the herbs and spices, with salt to taste. Heat to simmering point, cover, turn off the heat and allow to stand for 30 minutes to infuse, then strain.

Melt the butter in a saucepan. Stir in the flour and cook over low heat for 2–3 minutes, without browning. With the heat on the lowest setting, gradually add the flavoured milk, stirring constantly.

Increase the heat to moderate, stirring until the mixture boils and thickens to a coating consistency. Lower the heat when the mixture boils and simmer the sauce for 1–2 minutes, beating briskly to give the sauce a gloss. Stir in the cream, if used, and remove the sauce from the heat at once. Do not allow the sauce to come to the boil again. Add salt if required.

MAKES ABOUT 600 ml / 1 pint

Puddings & Desserts

Christmas Pudding, Plum Pudding and Vegetarian Plum Pudding vie for your attention with trifle, alcoholic jellies, syllabubs, crumbles, cobblers and much more, including the cheese course ... if you have room!

RICH CHRISTMAS PUDDING

butter for greasing
225 g / 8 oz plain flour
pinch of salt
5 ml / 1 tsp ground ginger
5 ml / 1 tsp mixed spice
5 ml / 1 tsp grated nutmeg
50 g / 2 oz blanched almonds, chopped
400 g / 14 oz soft dark brown sugar
225 g / 8 oz shredded suet
225 g / 8 oz sultanas
225 g / 8 oz currants
200 g / 7 oz seedless raisins
175 g / 6 oz cut mixed peel
175 g / 6 oz dried white breadcrumbs
6 eggs
75 ml / 5 tbsp stout
juice of 1 orange
50 ml / 2 fl oz brandy
125–250 ml / 4–9 fl oz milk

Grease four 600-ml / 1-pint pudding basins. Three-quarters fill four saucepans, each deep enough to hold a single pudding, with water.

Sift the flour, salt, ginger, mixed spice and nutmeg into a very large mixing bowl. Add the almonds, sugar, suet, dried fruit, peel and breadcrumbs.

In a second bowl, combine the eggs, stout, orange juice, brandy and 125 ml / 4 fl oz milk. Mix well.

Stir the liquid mixture into the dry ingredients, adding more milk if necessary to give a soft dropping consistency. Divide the mixture between the pudding basins, covering each with greased greaseproof paper and a floured cloth or foil. Secure with string.

Carefully lower the basins into the pans of boiling water. Cover the pans and lower the heat so that the water is kept at a steady simmer.

Cook the puddings for 6–7 hours, topping up each pan with boiling water as required. The pudding basins should be covered at all times with boiling water.

To store, cover each pudding with a clean dry cloth, wrap in greaseproof paper and store in a cool, dry place until required. To reheat, boil or steam each pudding for 1½–2 hours. Serve with Brandy Butter (page 194) or Brandy and Almond Butter (page 196).

EACH PUDDING SERVES SIX

STORING CHRISTMAS PUDDING

The large quantity of sugar and dried fruit together act as a preservative in Christmas pudding. After cooking, make sure that the pudding is dry and wrap it in clean paper, then place it in an airtight container or seal it in a polythene bag. Foil may be used as an outer covering, over paper, but it should not come in direct contact with the pudding as the fruit acid causes it to break down and disintegrate to a coarse foil powder which ruins the surface of the pudding. Kept in a cool, dry, place, Christmas pudding will remain excellent for up to a year. 'Feed' it occasionally with a little brandy.

PRESSURE COOKER TIP

Pour 1.5 litres / 2¾ pints boiling water into the pressure cooker. Stand one pudding on the trivet and steam it, without weights, for 20 minutes. Bring to 15 lb pressure and cook for 1¾ hours. Allow the pressure to reduce slowly. To reheat, cook at 15 lb pressure for 20 minutes, reduce pressure slowly and serve.

PLUM PUDDING

Christmas pudding became known as plum pudding in Tudor times, when dried plums (prunes) were the popular prime ingredient.

butter for greasing
100 g / 4 oz cooking apple
200 g / 7 oz dried figs, chopped
100 g / 4 oz currants
225 g / 8 oz seedless raisins
200 g / 7 oz blanched almonds, chopped
25 g / 1 oz shelled Brazil nuts, chopped
100 g / 4 oz pine kernels
175 g / 6 oz dried white breadcrumbs
5 ml / 1 tsp mixed spice
100 g / 4 oz soft light brown sugar
100 g / 4 oz cut mixed peel
pinch of salt
grated rind and juice of 1 lemon
100 g / 4 oz butter or margarine
100 g / 4 oz honey
3 eggs, beaten

Grease two 750-ml / 1¼-pint pudding basins. Prepare two steamers or three-quarter fill two saucepans with water. Each pan should hold one pudding.

Peel, core and chop the apple. Put it in a large mixing bowl with the dried fruits, nuts, breadcrumbs, spice, sugar, peel, salt and the lemon rind and juice.

Combine the butter and honey in a saucepan and warm gently until the butter has melted. Beat in the eggs.

Stir the liquid mixture into the dry ingredients and mix well. Spoon the mixture into the basins, cover with greased greaseproof paper and a floured cloth or foil. Secure with string.

Place the basins in the steamers or carefully lower them into the pans of boiling water. Cover the pans and lower the heat so that the water is kept at a steady simmer. Boil the puddings for 3 hours or steam for 3½–4 hours, topping up each pan with boiling water as required.

To store, cover each pudding with a clean dry cloth, wrap in greaseproof paper and store in a cool, dry place until required. To reheat, boil or steam each pudding for 1½–2 hours.

EACH PUDDING SERVES SIX

MRS BEETON'S TIP

Plum puddings are traditionally flamed when served. To do this, warm 30–45 ml / 2–3 tbsp brandy, either in a soup ladle over a low flame or in a measuring jug in the microwave for 15 seconds on High. Ignite the brandy (if warmed in a soup ladle it may well ignite spontaneously) and carefully pour it over the hot pudding. Do not use holly to decorate the top of a pudding that is to be flamed.

VEGETARIAN PLUM PUDDING

butter or margarine for greasing
200 g / 7 oz blanched almonds, chopped
25 g / 1 oz shelled Brazil nuts, chopped
100 g / 4 oz pine kernels
100 g / 4 oz cooking apple, chopped
200 g / 7 oz dried figs, chopped
100 g / 4 oz currants
200 g / 7 oz raisins
175 g / 6 oz day-old wholemeal breadcrumbs
1 tsp mixed spice
100 g / 4 oz soft light brown sugar
100 g / 4 oz mixed peel
pinch of salt
grated rind and juice of 1 lemon
100 g / 4 oz butter or margarine
100 g / 4 oz honey
3 eggs, beaten

Grease two 750-ml / 1¼-pint pudding basins. Mix together the nuts, apple, dried fruits, breadcrumbs, spice, sugar, peel, salt, lemon rind and juice.

Warm the butter or margarine and honey together until the fat melts, stir in the eggs and stir the mixture into the dry ingredients. Mix all together thoroughly.

Fill the prepared basins, leaving 2.5 cm / 1 in headspace, and cover with greased paper and a scalded and floured cloth (for boiling) or with greased paper or foil (for steaming), tying under the rim of the basin with string or twisting the edge. Place in a deep pan of boiling water and boil steadily for 3 hours, or half-steam for 3½–4 hours.

Store as for Plum Pudding (page 159). To reheat, boil or steam for 1½ –2 hours, or cook in the microwave on high setting for 7–9 minutes.

Serve with a sweet flavoured butter (pages 194–6), a custard sauce (pages 186–190), plain yoghurt, ice-cream or crème fraîche.

MAKES TWO SIX–EIGHT PORTION PUDDINGS

GINGER PUDDING

butter for greasing
200 g / 7 oz plain flour
5 ml / 1 tsp ground ginger
pinch of salt
5 ml / 1 tsp bicarbonate of soda
100 g / 4 oz shredded suet
75 g / 3 oz caster sugar
15 ml / 1 tbsp black treacle
1 egg, beaten
50–100 ml / 2–3½ fl oz milk

Grease a 1-litre / 1¾-pint pudding basin. Prepare a steamer or half fill a large saucepan with water and bring to the boil.

Sift the flour, ginger, salt and bicarbonate of soda into a mixing bowl. Add the suet and sugar. Mix lightly.

In a second bowl, beat the treacle and egg with 50 ml / 2 fl oz of the milk. Stir the liquid mixture into the dry ingredients, adding more milk if necessary to give a soft dropping consistency.

Spoon the mixture into the prepared basin, cover with greased greaseproof paper and foil and secure with string.

Put the pudding in the perforated part of the steamer, or stand it on an old saucer or plate in the pan of boiling water. The water should come halfway up the sides of the basin. Cover the pan tightly and steam the pudding over gently simmering water for 1¾–2 hours.

Serve from the basin or leave for 5–10 minutes at room temperature to firm up, then turn out on to a serving plate. Serve with Ginger Syrup Sauce (page 193) or Classic Egg Custard Sauce (page 190).

SERVES SIX

MRS BEETON'S TRIFLE

Plain whisked or creamed sponge cake, individual buns, or Madeira cake are ideal for this trifle. Originally, Mrs Beeton made her custard by using 8 eggs to thicken 600 ml / 1 pint milk, cooking it slowly over hot water. Using cornflour and egg yolks is more practical and it gives a creamier, less 'eggy' result.

4 slices of plain cake or individual cakes
6 almond macaroons
12 ratafias
175 ml / 6 fl oz sherry
30–45 ml / 2–3 tbsp brandy
60–90 ml / 4–6 tbsp raspberry or strawberry jam
grated rind of 1 lemon
25 g / 1 oz flaked almonds
300 ml / ½ pint double cream
30 ml / 2 tbsp icing sugar
candied and crystallized fruit and peel to decorate

CUSTARD
25 g / 1 oz cornflour
25 g / 1 oz caster sugar
4 egg yolks
5 ml / 1 tsp vanilla essence
600 ml / 1 pint milk

Place the sponge cakes in a glass dish. Add the macaroons and ratafias, pressing them down gently. Pour about 50 ml / 2 fl oz of the sherry into a basin and set it aside, then pour the rest over the biscuits and cake. Sprinkle with the brandy. Warm the jam in a small saucepan, then pour it evenly over the trifle base, spreading it lightly. Top with the lemon rind and almonds.

For the custard, blend the cornflour, caster sugar, egg yolks and vanilla to a smooth cream with a little of the milk. Heat the remaining milk until hot. Pour some of the milk on the egg mixture, stirring, then replace the mixture in the saucepan with the rest of the milk. Bring to the boil, stirring constantly, and simmer for 3 minutes.

Pour the custard over the trifle base and cover the surface with a piece of dampened greaseproof paper. Set aside to cool.

Add the cream and icing sugar to the reserved sherry and whip until the mixture stands in soft peaks. Swirl the cream over the top of the trifle and chill. Decorate with pieces of candied and crystallized fruit and peel before serving.

SERVES SIX

PINEAPPLE AND KIRSCH SALAD

2 small pineapples
100 g / 4 oz black grapes
1 banana
1 pear
15 ml / 1 tbsp lemon juice
30–45 ml / 2–3 tbsp kirsch
sugar

Cut the pineapples in half lengthways. Cut out the cores, then scoop out the flesh, using first a knife, then a spoon, but taking care to keep the shells intact. Discard the cores, and working over a bowl to catch the juice, chop the flesh.

Add the pineapple flesh to the bowl. Halve the grapes and remove the pips. Add to the pineapple mixture. Peel and slice the banana; peel, core, and slice the pear. Put the lemon juice in a shallow bowl, add the pear and banana slices and toss both fruits before adding to the pineapple and grapes.

Mix all the fruit together, pour the kirsch over and sweeten to taste with the sugar. Pile the fruit back into the pineapple shells and chill until required.

SERVES FOUR

MRS BEETON'S ORANGE SALAD

5 oranges
50 g / 2 oz caster sugar (or to taste)
2.5 ml / ½ tsp ground mixed spice
100 g / 4 oz muscatel raisins
60 ml / 4 tbsp brandy

Peel four oranges, removing all pith. Slice them, discarding the pips. Mix the sugar and spice in a bowl. Layer the orange slices in a serving dish, sprinkling each layer with the sugar mixture and raisins.

Squeeze the juice from the remaining orange and sprinkle it over the salad. Pour over the brandy, cover and leave to macerate for 24 hours before serving.

SERVES FOUR

PEARS IN WINE

100 g / 4 oz sugar
30 ml / 2 tbsp redcurrant jelly
1.5 cm / ¾ inch cinnamon stick
4 large ripe cooking pears (about 450 g / 1 lb)
250 ml / 9 fl oz red wine
25 g / 1 oz flaked almonds

Combine the sugar, redcurrant jelly and cinnamon stick in a saucepan wide enough to hold all the pears upright so that they fit snugly and will not fall over. Add 250 ml / 9 fl oz water and heat gently, stirring constantly, until the sugar and jelly have dissolved.

Peel the pears, leaving the stalks in place. Carefully remove as much core as possible without breaking the fruit. Stand them upright in the pan, cover, and simmer gently for 15 minutes. Add the wine and cook, uncovered, for 15 minutes more. Remove them gently with a slotted spoon and arrange on a serving dish.

Remove the cinnamon stick from the pan and add the almonds. Boil the liquid remaining in the pan rapidly until it is reduced to a thin syrup. Pour the syrup over the pears and serve warm. This dessert can also be served cold. Pour the hot syrup over the pears, leave to cool, then chill before serving.

SERVES FOUR

BANANAS IN RUM

45 ml / 3 tbsp soft light brown sugar
2.5 ml / ½ tsp ground cinnamon
4 large bananas
25 g / 1 oz butter
45–60 ml / 3–4 tbsp rum
150 ml / ¼ pint double cream to serve

Mix the sugar and cinnamon in a shallow dish. Cut the bananas in half length-ways and dredge them in the sugar and cinnamon mixture.

Melt the butter in a frying pan and fry the bananas, flat side down, for 1–2 minutes or until lightly browned underneath. Turn them over carefully, sprinkle with any remaining sugar and cinnamon and continue frying.

When the bananas are soft but not mushy, pour the rum over them. Tilt the pan and baste the bananas, then ignite the rum; baste again. Scrape any caramelized sugar from the base of the pan and stir it into the rum sauce. Shake the pan gently until the flames die down. Arrange the bananas on warmed plates, pour the rum sauce over the top and serve with cream.

SERVES FOUR

PLUMS WITH PORT

1 kg / 2¼ lb firm plums
100–150 g / 4–5 oz soft light brown sugar
150 ml / ¼ pint port

Set the oven at 150°C / 300°F / gas 2. Cut the plums neatly in half and remove the stones.

Put the plums into a baking dish or casserole, sprinkle with the sugar (the amount required will depend on the sweetness of the plums) and pour the port over the top.

Cover the dish securely with a lid or foil and bake for 45–60 minutes, or until the plums are tender. Serve hot or lightly chilled.

SERVES SIX

MICROWAVE TIP

Cook in a covered dish for 10-12 minutes on High, stirring gently once or twice during the cooking time.

ORANGES IN CARAMEL SAUCE

6 oranges
200 g / 7 oz sugar
50–125 ml / 2–4 fl oz chilled orange juice

Using a vegetable peeler, remove the rind from 1 orange, taking care not to include any of the bitter pith. Cut the rind into strips with a sharp knife. Bring a small saucepan of water to the boil, add the orange strips and cook for 1 minute, then drain and set aside on absorbent kitchen paper.

Carefully peel the remaining oranges, leaving them whole. Remove the pith from all the oranges and place the fruit in a heatproof bowl.

Put the sugar in a saucepan with 125 ml / 4 fl oz water. Heat gently, stirring until the sugar has dissolved, then bring to the boil and boil rapidly, without stirring, until the syrup turns a golden caramel colour. Remove from the heat and carefully add the orange juice. Replace over the heat and stir until just blended, then add the reserved orange rind.

Pour the hot caramel sauce over the oranges and chill for at least 3 hours before serving.

SERVES SIX

FREEZER TIP

Cool the oranges quickly in the sauce, place in a rigid container, cover and freeze for up to 12 months. Remember to allow a little headspace in the top of the container, as the syrup will expand upon freezing. Thaw, covered, in the refrigerator for about 6 hours.

PORT WINE JELLY

25 ml / 5 tsp gelatine
50 g / 2 oz sugar
30 ml / 2 tbsp redcurrant jelly
250 ml / 9 fl oz port
few drops of red food colouring

Place 30 ml /2 tbsp water in a small bowl and sprinkle the gelatine on to the liquid. Set aside for 15 minutes until the gelatine is spongy. Stand the bowl over a saucepan of hot water and stir the gelatine until it has dissolved.

Combine the sugar and redcurrant jelly in a pan. Add 400 ml / 14 fl oz water and heat gently, stirring constantly, until all the sugar has dissolved.

Add the gelatine liquid to the syrup and stir in the port and food colouring. Pour through a strainer lined with a single thickness of scalded fine cotton or muslin into a wetted 900-ml / 1½-pint mould. Chill until set.

SERVES SIX

WINE SYLLABUB

This syllabub has a frothy head, with the lemon juice and wine settling in the bottom of the glasses.

200 ml / 7 fl oz double cream
2 egg whites
75 g / 3 oz caster sugar
juice of ½ lemon
100 ml / 3½ fl oz sweet white wine or sherry
crystallized lemon slices to decorate

In a large bowl, whip the cream until it just holds its shape. Put the egg whites in a clean, grease-free mixing bowl and whisk until they form soft peaks. Fold the sugar into the egg whites, then gradually add the lemon juice and wine or sherry.

Fold the egg white mixture into the whipped cream. Pour into glasses and refrigerate for about 2 hours. Remove 20 minutes before serving. Serve decorated with the crystallized lemon slices.

SERVES FOUR

CIDER SYLLABUB

A syllabub was originally a sweet, frothy drink made with cider or mead mixed with milk straight from the cow. Mrs Beeton's original syllabub recipe combined 600 ml / 1 pint of sherry or white wine with 900 ml / 1½ pints of fresh, frothy milk. Nutmeg or cinnamon and sugar was stirred in, and clotted cream may have been added. When cider was used instead of wine, brandy was added to enrich the syllabub. It is now a rich creamy dessert, often made light and frothy by the addition of egg whites.

grated rind and juice of ½ lemon
50 g / 2 oz caster sugar
125 ml / 4 fl oz sweet cider
15 ml / 1 tbsp brandy
250 ml / 9 fl oz double cream

In a large bowl, mix the lemon rind and juice with the caster sugar, cider and brandy. Stir until the sugar is dissolved.

Put the cream in a mixing bowl. Whip until it stands in stiff peaks. Gradually fold in the lemon and cider mixture. Pour the mixture into stemmed glasses and refrigerate for about 2 hours. Remove 20 minutes before serving to allow the flavours to 'ripen'.

SERVES FOUR

FROSTED APPLES

oil for greasing
6 cooking apples (about 800 g / 1¾ lb)
30 ml / 2 tbsp lemon juice
100 g / 4 oz granulated sugar
15 ml / 1 tbsp fine-cut marmalade
2.5 cm / 1 inch cinnamon stick
2 cloves
2 egg whites
100 g / 4 oz caster sugar, plus extra for dusting

DECORATION
125 ml / 4 fl oz double cream
glacé cherries
angelica

Line a large baking sheet with greaseproof paper or non-stick baking parchment. Oil the lining paper. Set the oven at 180°C / 350°F / gas 4.

Wash, core and peel the apples, leaving them whole. Reserve the peelings. Brush the apples all over with the lemon juice to preserve the colour.

Combine the granulated sugar, marmalade, cinnamon stick, cloves and apple peelings in a large saucepan. Stir in 250 ml / 9 fl oz water. Heat gently, stirring occasionally, until the sugar and marmalade have melted, then boil for 2–3 minutes without stirring to make a thin syrup.

Place the apples in a baking dish and strain the syrup over them. Cover with a lid or foil and bake for about 30 minutes or until the apples are just tender. Lower the oven temperature to 120°C / 250°F / gas ½.

Using a slotted spoon, carefully remove the apples from the syrup, dry well on absorbent kitchen paper, then place on the prepared baking sheet.

Whisk the egg whites in a clean, grease-free bowl until they form stiff peaks, then gradually whisk in the caster sugar, a teaspoon at a time (see Mrs Beeton's Tip).

Coat each apple completely with the meringue, and dust lightly with caster sugar. Return to the oven and bake for about 1½ hours or until the meringue is firm and very lightly coloured. Remove from the oven and leave to cool.

In a bowl, whip the cream until it just holds its shape. Pile a spoonful on top of each apple and decorate with small pieces of cherry and angelica. Serve the apples on a bed of whipped cream in individual bowls, or with the cold baking syrup poured over them.

SERVES SIX

MRS BEETON'S TIP

If using an electric whisk to make the meringue, whisk in all the sugar. If whisking by hand, however, whisk in only half the sugar and fold in the rest.

DRIED FRUIT COMPOTE

100 g / 4 oz dried apricots
100 g / 4 oz prunes
100 g / 4 oz dried figs
50 g / 2 oz dried apple rings
30 ml / 2 tbsp liquid honey
2.5 cm / 1 inch cinnamon stick
2 cloves
pared rind and juice of ½ lemon
50 g / 2 oz raisins
50 g / 2 oz flaked almonds, toasted

Combine the apricots, prunes and figs in a bowl. Add water to cover. Put the apples in separate bowl with water to cover and leave both bowls to soak overnight.

Next day, place the honey in a saucepan with 600 ml / 1 pint water. Add the cinnamon stick, cloves and lemon rind. Bring to the boil. Stir in the lemon juice.

Drain both bowls of soaked fruit. Add the mixed fruit to the pan, cover and simmer for 10 minutes. Stir in the drained apples and simmer for 10 minutes more, then add the raisins and simmer for 2–3 minutes. Discard the cinnamon, cloves and lemon rind.

Spoon the compote into a serving dish and sprinkle with the almonds. Serve warm or cold.

SERVES SIX

MICROWAVE TIP

There is no need to presoak the dried fruit. Make the honey syrup in a large bowl, using 450 ml/ ¾ pint water. Microwave on High for about 4 minutes, then stir in all the dried fruit with the cinnamon, cloves and lemon rind. Cover and cook on High for 15–20 minutes or until all the fruit is soft. Stir several times during cooking, each time pressing the fruit down into the syrup.

SPICED RHUBARB COBBLER

Scones flavoured with spices and dried fruit make a hearty topping for tart stewed rhubarb.

675 g / 1½ lb rhubarb, trimmed and sliced
100 g / 4 oz sugar

TOPPING
175 g / 6 oz self-raising flour
5 ml / 1 tsp baking powder
40 g / 1½ oz butter or margarine
30 ml / 2 tbsp sugar
5 ml / 1 tsp ground mixed spice
50 g / 2 oz mixed dried fruit
grated rind of 1 orange (optional)
about 75 ml / 3 fl oz milk, plus extra for brushing

Place the rhubarb and sugar in a heavy-bottomed saucepan and cook gently until the juice begins to run from the fruit and the sugar dissolves. Stirring occasionally, continue to cook the rhubarb gently for 15–20 minutes, until tender. Transfer to an ovenproof dish.

Set the oven at 230°C / 450°F / gas 8. Make the topping. Sift the flour into a bowl with the baking powder. Rub in the butter or margarine until the mixture resembles fine breadcrumbs, then stir in the sugar, spice, dried fruit and orange rind (if used). Mix in enough of the milk to make a soft dough.

Turn the dough out on to a lightly floured surface, knead it gently into a ball and roll it out to about 1 cm / ½ inch thick. Use a 5-cm / 2-inch round cutter to cut out scones. Arrange the scones on top of the fruit.

Brush the scones with milk and bake for 12–15 minutes, until risen and golden.

SERVES FOUR

NUTTY PLUM CRUMBLE

Tangy plums and toasted hazelnuts make a tasty combination in this tempting pudding. Apples, rhubarb, gooseberries, or a mixture of fruit may be used instead of the plums.

675 g / 1½ lb, plums, halved and stoned
50 g / 2 oz sugar

TOPPING
175 g / 6 oz plain flour
75 g / 3 oz butter or margarine
25 g / 1 oz demerara sugar
5 ml / 1 tsp ground cinnamon
75 g / 3 oz hazelnuts, toasted and chopped

Set the oven at 180°C / 350°F / gas 4. Place the plums in an ovenproof dish and sprinkle with the sugar.

Make the topping. Sift the flour into a mixing bowl and rub in the butter or margarine until the mixture resembles fine breadcrumbs. Stir in the sugar, cinnamon and hazelnuts.

Sprinkle the topping evenly over the plums, pressing it down very lightly. Bake the crumble for about 45 minutes, until the topping is golden brown and the plums are cooked. Serve with custard (pages 186–190), cream or vanilla ice cream.

SERVES FOUR TO SIX

APPLE CRUMBLE

butter for greasing
675 g / 1½ lb cooking apples
100 g / 4 oz granulated sugar
grated rind of 1 lemon
150 g / 5 oz plain flour
75 g / 3 oz butter or margarine
75 g / 3 oz caster sugar
1.25 ml / ¼ tsp ground ginger

Grease a 1-litre / 1¾-pint pie dish. Set the oven at 180°C / 350°F / gas 4. Peel and core the apples. Slice into a saucepan and add the granulated sugar and lemon rind. Stir in 50 ml / 2 fl oz water, cover the pan and cook until the apples are soft. Spoon the apple mixture into the prepared dish and set aside.

Put the flour into a mixing bowl and rub in the butter or margarine until the mixture resembles fine breadcrumbs. Add the caster sugar and ginger and stir well. Sprinkle the mixture over the apples and press down lightly. Bake for 30–40 minutes until the crumble topping is golden brown.

SERVES SIX

VARIATIONS

- Instead of apples, use 675 g / 1½ lb damsons, gooseberries, pears, plums, rhubarb or raspberries.

MICROWAVE TIP

Put the apple mixture in a large bowl, adding only 30 ml / 2 tbsp water, cover and cook for 7 minutes on High. Add the crumble topping and cook for 4 minutes more, then brown the topping under a preheated grill.

BROWN BETTY

butter for greasing
1 kg / 2¼ lb cooking apples
150 g / 5 oz dried wholewheat breadcrumbs
grated rind and juice of 1 lemon
60 ml / 4 tbsp golden syrup
100 g / 4 oz demerara sugar

Grease a 1-litre / 1¾-pint pie dish. Set the oven at 160°C / 325°F / gas 3.

Peel and core the apples. Slice them thinly into a bowl. Coat the prepared pie dish with a thin layer of breadcrumbs, then fill with alternate layers of apples, lemon rind and breadcrumbs. Put the syrup, sugar and lemon juice into a saucepan. Add 30 ml / 2 tbsp water. Heat until the syrup has dissolved, then pour the mixture over the layered pudding. Bake for 1–1¼ hours until the pudding is brown and the apple cooked. Serve with single cream or Vanilla Custard (page 188).

SERVES SIX

MRS BEETON'S TIP

Use a tablespoon dipped in boiling water to measure the golden syrup. The syrup will slide off easily.

BAKED APPLES

6 cooking apples
75 g / 3 oz sultanas, chopped
50 g / 2 oz demerara sugar

Wash and core the apples. Cut around the skin of each apple with the tip of a sharp knife two-thirds of the way up from the base. Put the apples into an oven-proof dish, and fill the centres with the chopped sultanas.

Sprinkle the demerara sugar on top of the apples and pour 75 ml / 5 tbsp water around them. Bake for 45–60 minutes, depending on the cooking quality and size of the apples.

Serve accompanied by Vanilla Custard (page 188), vanilla ice cream, Brandy Butter (page 194) or with whipped cream.

SERVES SIX

VARIATIONS

- Fill the apple cavities with a mixture of 50 g / 2 oz Barbados or other raw sugar and 50 g / 2 oz butter, or use blackcurrant, raspberry, strawberry or apricot jam, or marmalade. Instead of sultanas, chopped stoned dates, raisins or currants could be used. A topping of toasted almonds looks effective and tastes delicious.

MICROWAVE TIP

Baked apples cook superbly in the microwave. Prepare as suggested above, but reduce the amount of water to 30 ml / 2 tsp. Cook for 10–12 minutes on High.

BAKED APPLES STUFFED WITH RICE AND NUTS

6 medium cooking apples
25 g / 1 oz flaked almonds or other nuts
40 g / 1½ oz seedless raisins
25–50 g / 1–2 oz boiled rice (preferably boiled in milk)
50 g / 2 oz sugar or to taste
1 egg, beaten
30 ml / 2 tbsp butter
raspberry or blackcurrant syrup

Set the oven at 190°C / 375°F / gas 5. Wash and core the apples but do not peel them. With a small rounded spoon, hollow out part of the flesh surrounding the core hole. Do not break the outside skin.

In a bowl, mix together the nuts, raisins and rice, using enough rice to make a stuffing for all the apples. Add the sugar, with enough egg to bind the mixture. Melt the butter and stir it into the mixture.

Fill the apples with the rice mixture. Place in a roasting tin and add hot water to a depth of 5 mm / ¼ inch. Bake for 40 minutes or until the apples are tender. Remove the roasting tin from the oven and transfer the apples to a warmed serving platter, using a slotted spoon. Warm the fruit syrup and pour it over the apples.

MICROWAVE TIP

The rice may be cooked in the microwave. Place 50 g / 2 oz pudding rice in a large bowl with 30 ml / 2 tbsp sugar. Stir in 600 ml / 1 pint water, cover and cook on High for 25 minutes. Stir well, then stir in 300 ml / ½ pint top-of-the-milk or single cream. Use 25–50 g / 1–2 oz of the cooked rice for the above pudding and reserve the remainder.

BREAD AND BUTTER PUDDING

When the weather is dull and dreary, lift the spirits with this comforting old favourite.

butter for greasing
4 thin slices of bread (about 100 g / 4 oz)
25 g / 1 oz butter
50 g / 2 oz sultanas or currants
pinch of ground nutmeg or cinnamon
400 ml / 14 fl oz milk
2 eggs
25 g / 1 oz granulated sugar

Grease a 1-litre / 1¾-pint pie dish. Cut the crusts off the bread and spread the slices with the butter. Cut the bread into squares or triangles and arrange in alternate layers, buttered side up, with the sultanas or currants. Sprinkle each layer lightly with nutmeg or cinnamon. Arrange the top layer of bread in an attractive pattern.

Warm the milk in a saucepan to about 65°C / 150°F. Do not let it approach boiling point. Put the eggs in a bowl. Add most of the sugar. Beat with a fork and stir in the milk. Strain the custard mixture over the bread, sprinkle some nutmeg and the remaining sugar on top, and leave to stand for 30 minutes. Set the oven at 180°C / 350°F / gas 4. Bake for 30–40 minutes until the custard is set and the top is lightly browned.

SERVES FOUR

PRESSURE COOKER TIP

Use a dish that fits in the pressure cooker. Cover the pudding with foil or greased greaseproof paper, tied down securely. Cook at 15 lb pressure for 9 minutes. Reduce pressure slowly, then brown the pudding under the grill.

JAPANESE PLOMBIÈRE

A plombière is an ice cream mixture containing almonds or chestnuts. It may be frozen in a decorative mould but is more often scooped into balls and piled up to form a pyramid. It is often served with a sauce poured over the top.

50 g / 2 oz apricot jam
few drops of lemon juice
8 egg yolks
100 g / 4 oz caster sugar
500 ml / 18 fl oz single cream
2.5 ml / ½ tsp vanilla essence
100 g / 4 oz ground almonds
250 ml / 9 fl oz double cream
100 g / 4 oz almond macaroons, crushed
12 ratafias to decorate

Turn the freezing compartment or freezer to the coldest setting about 1 hour before making the ice cream.

Make an apricot marmalade by boiling the apricot jam in a small saucepan with a few drops of lemon juice until thick. Keep a little aside for decoration and sieve the rest into a bowl.

Combine the egg yolks and caster sugar in a deep bowl and beat together until very thick. Put the single cream in a saucepan and bring slowly to the boil. Pour the cream over the yolks and sugar, stirring well. Return the mixture to the clean pan. Cook, stirring constantly, until the custard thickens. Do not allow it to boil. Pour the thickened custard into a large bowl and stir in the sieved apricot marmalade, the vanilla essence and the ground almonds. Cover closely with dampened greaseproof paper and cool.

In a bowl, whip the double cream to the same consistency as the custard. Fold it into the custard, with the crushed macaroons. Spoon the mixture into a suitable container for freezing (a bowl that is deep enough to allow the ice cream to be scooped is ideal). Freeze the mixture until firm.

To serve, scoop the ice cream into balls and arrange them as a pyramid on a chilled plate. Drizzle the reserved apricot marmalade over the top and decorate with the ratafias.

SERVES SIX TO EIGHT

MICROWAVE TIP

The apricot marmalade may be prepared in a small bowl in the microwave. It will only require about 30 seconds on High. Reheat it, if necessary, before pouring it over the ice cream pyramid.

VANILLA PLOMBIÈRE

700 ml / 1¼ pints vanilla ice cream
125 ml / 4 fl oz double cream
50 g / 2 oz flaked almonds

In a bowl, whip the cream to soft peaks. Beat the ice cream until smooth, scraping off any ice crystals, then fold in the whipped cream and almonds. Spoon into a suitable container, cover and freeze the ice cream until firm.

If the ice cream has been made in a mould or basin, turn it out on to a chilled plate and transfer it to the refrigerator about 15 minutes before serving, to allow it to soften and 'ripen'. If a plastic box or bowl has been used, scoop the ice cream into balls and form these into a pyramid on a dish.

SERVES SIX

BOMBE TORTONI

This is absurdly easy to make, yet it makes an impressive finale.

300 ml / ½ pint double cream
150 ml / ¼ pint single cream
50 g / 2 oz icing sugar, sifted
2.5 ml / ½ tsp vanilla essence
2 egg whites
100 g / 4 oz hazelnut biscuits or ratafias, crushed
30 ml / 2 tbsp sherry

Turn the freezing compartment or freezer to the coldest setting about 1 hour before making the bombe. Lightly oil a 1.25-litre / 2¼-pint bombe mould or pudding basin.

Combine the creams in a large bowl and whip until thick, adding half the icing sugar. Add the vanilla essence.

In a clean, grease-free bowl whisk the egg whites until stiff. Fold in the remaining icing sugar.

Lightly fold the meringue mixture into the whipped cream. Stir in the hazelnut biscuits and sherry. Spoon the mixture into the prepared mould.

Put the lid on the bombe mould or cover the basin with foil. Freeze until firm, then return the freezer to the normal setting. To turn out, dip the mould or basin in cold water, and invert on to a chilled serving dish. Transfer to the refrigerator 15 minutes before serving to allow the ice cream to soften and 'ripen'.

SERVES SIX TO EIGHT

VARIATIONS

- Try crushed ginger biscuits with coffee liqueur instead of sherry, or crumbled meringue with cherry brandy.

PLANNING A CHEESE COURSE

'A celebrated gourmand remarked that a dinner without cheese is like a woman with one eye.' Isabella Beeton

A cheese course typically features three or four cheeses, served on an open board or platter that can be passed around your guests. Selecting the cheeses is a great opportunity for tasting sessions at your delicatessen counter. A variety of strengths and textures works well; for example, a soft cheese (such as a goat's cheese), a semi-soft cheese (such as Port Salut or Camembert), a hard cheese (such as Applewood Smoked Cheddar), a crumbly white cheese (such as Lancashire or Wensleydale) or a blue cheese (such as strong-tasting Stilton or mild Dolcelatte).

- Serve cheese unwrapped and at room temperature. Arrange the cheese for serving, ensuring there is enough space around each cheese to cut it, and loosely cover by a clean tea towel.
- If you're planning for a large number of guests, provide more than one platter of the same cheeses.
- Provide each guest with a salad or bread plate to put the cheese on as it comes around.
- Special cheese knives are available, but the important thing is to provide knives that will allow for each cheese with a different texture – a sharp knife for semi-hard or hard cheeses and a butter knife for soft cheese. Slices ideally follow the natural lines of the cheese, or are taken like slices of cake from a round cheese.

- Serve crackers, water biscuits, oat cakes and/or interesting breads (those with nuts or fruit make excellent accompaniments). Also provide spreadable butter and margarine.
- If your meal has been relatively light, you might consider extra accompaniments to your cheese course such as grapes, sharp apples, figs, olives, cornichons, chutneys, flavoured oils, mustards, toasted seeds and nuts such as walnuts, or traditional pickled walnuts. It is a good idea to contrast flavours and textures. Try tart apple slices with mild creamy or plain salty cheeses; fresh figs with blue cheese. The region a cheese is from often suggests perfect partners: for example, Spanish Manchego is often teamed with a traditional quince jelly or almonds and sherry, and that Christmas favourite, British Stilton, is fantastic with port.
- A reputable cheese merchant is invaluable in giving advice on selection, combination and storage of cheeses, providing tasting samples, taking on board your own feedback and refining your serving ideas.

Sweet Sauces & Butters

A range of custards, chocolate- ginger- and alcohol-based sauces, caramel and brandy butter enhance your puddings and desserts and ensure that they are truly memorable.

CRÈME ANGLAISE

The classic egg custard sauce; and an essential ingredient of many desserts.

250 ml / 9 fl oz milk
few drops of vanilla essence or a strip of lemon rind
3 egg yolks
50 g / 2 oz caster sugar

Combine the milk and chosen flavouring in a saucepan. Warm gently but do not allow to boil.

In a bowl, beat the egg yolks and sugar together until creamy. Remove the lemon rind, if used, from the saucepan and add the milk to the eggs.

Strain the custard into a double saucepan or a heatproof bowl placed over a saucepan of simmering water. Cook, stirring constantly, until the custard thickens and coats the back of the spoon. Serve hot or cold.

MAKES 300 ml / ½ PINT

VARIATIONS

- **Liqueur Sauce** Stir 125 ml / 4 fl oz lightly whipped double cream and 30 ml / 2 tbsp orange-flavoured liqueur into the sauce.
- **Chocolate Custard Sauce** Use vanilla essence instead of lemon rind and add 100 g / 4 oz coarsely grated plain chocolate to the milk. Warm until the chocolate melts, stir, then add to the egg yolks and proceed as in the main recipe.

CORNFLOUR CUSTARD SAUCE

15 ml / 1 tbsp cornflour
250ml / 9 fl oz milk
1 egg yolk
15 ml / 1 tbsp sugar
few drops of vanilla essence

Mix the cornflour with a little of the cold milk in a large bowl. Bring the rest of the milk to the boil in a saucepan, then stir into the blended mixture. Return the mixture to the clean pan.

Bring the cornflour mixture to the boil and boil for 3 minutes to cook the cornflour. Remove from the heat.

When the mixture has cooled a little, stir in the egg yolk and sugar. Return to low heat and cook, stirring carefully, until the sauce thickens. Do not let it boil. Flavour with a few drops of vanilla essence and pour into a jug.

MAKES ABOUT 250 ml / 9 fl oz

MICROWAVE TIP

Mix the cornflour with all the milk in a bowl. Cook on High for 3–5 minutes, whisking twice. Whisk well, then whisk in the yolk, sugar and vanilla. Cook for a further 30–45 seconds on High.

CREAM CUSTARD SAUCE

4 egg yolks or 2 whole eggs
50 g / 2 oz caster sugar
125 ml / 4 fl oz milk
grated rind of 1 orange
125 ml / 4 fl oz single cream

In a mixing bowl, beat the egg yolks or the whole eggs with the sugar and milk. Stir in the orange rind and cream. Pour into a double saucepan or into a heat-proof bowl placed over a saucepan of simmering water. Cook, stirring all the time, until the sauce thickens. Serve hot or cold.

MAKES ABOUT 250 ml / 9 fl oz

MRS BEETON'S TIP

Do not allow the sauce to boil or it will curdle.

VANILLA CUSTARD

Adding cornflour stabilizes the custard and makes it less inclined to curdle.

10 ml / 2 tsp cornflour
500 ml / 18 fl oz milk
25 g / 1 oz caster sugar
2 eggs
vanilla essence

In a bowl, mix the cornflour to a smooth paste with a little of the cold milk. Heat the rest of the milk in a saucepan and when hot pour it on to the blended cornflour, stirring.

Return to the mixture to the pan, bring to the boil and boil for 1–2 minutes, stirring all the time, to cook the cornflour. Remove from the heat and stir in the sugar. Leave to cool.

Beat the eggs together lightly in a small bowl. Add a little of the cooked cornflour mixture, stir well, then pour into the pan. Heat gently for a few minutes until the custard has thickened, stirring all the time. Do not boil. Stir in a few drops of vanilla essence.

Serve hot or cold as an accompaniment to a pudding or pie.

MAKES ABOUT 600 ml / 1 pint

SIMPLE CUSTARD SAUCE

The addition of cornflour makes it unnecessary to use a double saucepan to make this sauce, provided care is taken to avoid excessive heat and the custard is constantly stirred.

500 ml / 18 fl oz milk
few drops of vanilla essence
6 egg yolks
100 g / 4 oz caster sugar
10 ml / 2 tsp cornflour

Combine the milk and vanilla essence in a saucepan. Warm gently but do not allow to boil.

In a bowl, beat the egg yolks, sugar and cornflour together until creamy. Add the warm milk.

Strain the mixture back into the clean pan and cook, stirring constantly, until the custard thickens and coats the back of the spoon. Serve hot or cold.

MAKES ABOUT 600 ml / 1 pint

CLASSIC EGG CUSTARD SAUCE

500 ml / 18 fl oz milk
few drops of vanilla essence or other flavouring
6 egg yolks
100 g / 4 oz caster sugar

Put the milk in a saucepan with the vanilla or other flavouring. Warm gently but do not let the liquid boil. If a solid flavouring such as a strip of citrus rind is used, allow it to infuse in the milk for 5 minutes, then remove.

In a bowl, beat the egg yolks and sugar together until creamy. Add the warm milk to the egg mixture.

Strain the mixture into a double saucepan or a heatproof bowl placed over a saucepan of simmering water. Cook, stirring constantly with a wooden spoon for 20–30 minutes, until the custard thickens and coats the back of the spoon. Take care not to let the custard curdle. Serve hot or cold.

MAKES ABOUT 500 ml / 18 fl oz

VARIATIONS

- **Classic Lemon Custard** Infuse a thin strip of lemon rind in the milk, removing it before adding to the eggs.
- **Classic Orange Custard** Substitute orange for lemon rind.
- **Classic Liqueur Custard** Add 15 ml / 1 tbsp kirsch or curaçao at the end of the cooking time.

PLUM PUDDING SAUCE

A thin sauce with a rich, buttery flavour to make a potent impression on Christmas pudding or a variety of other desserts.

100 g / 4 oz caster sugar
75 ml / 3 fl oz brandy
50 g / 2 oz unsalted butter, diced
175 ml / 6 fl oz Madeira

Put the sugar in a heatproof bowl with 30 ml / 2 tbsp of the brandy. Add the butter. Set over simmering water and stir until the mixture is smooth. Gradually stir in the rest of the brandy with the Madeira and warm through. Either serve over the pudding or in a sauceboat.

MAKES 350 ml / 12 fl oz

CARAMEL

200 g / 7 oz caster sugar

Put the sugar in a heavy-bottomed saucepan. Add 125 ml / 4 fl oz water and stir over low heat for 3–4 minutes until the sugar has dissolved. Increase the heat and boil, without stirring, until the syrup is a light golden brown. Do not allow it to darken too much or it will taste bitter.

Immediately plunge the bottom of the pan into warm water to prevent further cooking. Allow the caramel mixture to cool slightly, then carefully add a further 75 ml / 3 fl oz water. Return the pan to a low heat and stir constantly until the mixture becomes smooth. Remove from the heat. cool slightly, then use as required.

SERVES FOUR

CHOCOLATE CREAM SAUCE

Add a touch of luxury to rice pudding, poached pears or ice cream with this sauce. When cold, the sauce thickens enough to be used as a soft filling for éclairs or profiteroles.

75 g / 3 oz plain chocolate, roughly grated
15 ml / 1 tbsp butter
15 ml / 1 tbsp single cream
5 ml / 1 tsp vanilla essence

Put the grated chocolate in a heatproof bowl with the butter. Add 60 ml / 4 tbsp water. Stand the bowl over a saucepan of simmering water and stir until the chocolate and butter have melted.

When the chocolate mixture is smooth, remove from the heat and immediately stir in the cream and vanilla essence. Serve at once.

MAKES ABOUT 125 ml / 4 fl oz

MICROWAVE TIP

Combine the chocolate, butter and water in a bowl. Heat on High for about 1 minute, stirring once, until the chocolate has melted. Finish as above.

GINGER SYRUP SAUCE

Warm a winter's evening with this sauce poured over Ginger Pudding (page 161).

strip of lemon rind
piece of fresh root ginger
125 ml / 4 fl oz ginger syrup (from jar of preserved ginger)
100 g / 4 oz soft light brown sugar, golden syrup or honey
5 ml / 1 tsp lemon juice
10 ml / 2 tsp arrowroot
2.5 ml / ½ tsp ground ginger
15 ml / 1 tbsp preserved ginger, chopped

Put the lemon rind, root ginger and syrup into a saucepan. Add 125 ml / 4 fl oz water. Heat to boiling point. Lower the heat and simmer gently for 15 minutes.

Remove the lemon rind and root ginger. Add the brown sugar, syrup or honey, bring the mixture to the boil and boil for 5 minutes. Stir in the lemon juice.

In a cup, mix the arrowroot and ground ginger with a little cold water until smooth. Stir the arrowroot mixture into the hot liquid. Heat gently until the liquid thickens, stirring all the time.

Add the preserved ginger to the sauce and simmer for 2–3 minutes. Serve hot.

MAKES ABOUT 300 ml / ½ pint

MRS BEETON'S TIP

The syrup in a jar of preserved ginger makes a delicious addition to gingerbreads, steamed puddings and pancakes.

SWEET BUTTERS

Sweet butters may be used to top pancakes, waffles, crumpets or drop scones. They are also used on fruit puddings, the best example being brandy butter, which is traditionally served with Christmas pudding.

BRANDY BUTTER

50 g / 2 oz butter
100 g / 4 oz caster sugar
15–30 ml / 1–2 tbsp brandy

In a bowl, cream the butter until soft. Gradually beat in the sugar until the mixture is pale and light. Work in the brandy, a little at a time, taking care not to allow the mixture to curdle. Chill before using. If the mixture has separated slightly after standing, beat well before serving.

MAKES ABOUT 150 g / 5 oz

VARIATIONS

- **Sherry Butter** Make as for Brandy Butter but substitute sherry for the brandy. Add a stiffly beaten egg white, if a softer texture is preferred.
- **Vanilla Butter** Make as for Brandy Butter but substitute 5 ml / 1 tsp vanilla essence for the brandy.
- **Orange or Lemon Butter** Cream the grated rind of 1 orange or ½ lemon with the butter and sugar. then gradually beat in 15 ml / 1 tbsp orange juice or 5 ml / 1 tsp lemon juice. Omit the brandy.

ORANGE LIQUEUR BUTTER

grated rind of 2 oranges
4 sugar lumps
150 g / 5 oz butter, softened
25 g / 1 oz caster sugar
15 ml / 1 tbsp orange juice, strained
20 ml / 4 tsp Cointreau

Put the orange rind in a bowl and mix it with the sugar lumps. Work in the butter and caster sugar until well blended.

Stir in the juice and liqueur gradually, until fully absorbed. Use at once, or pot and chill (see Mrs Beeton's Tip).

MAKES ABOUT 175 g / 6 oz

MRS BEETON'S TIP

Pots of Orange Liqueur Butter make good gifts. Press the butter into small pots or cartons (mini yogurt pots are perfect) and cover. Chill in the refrigerator. Do not freeze.

BRANDY AND ALMOND BUTTER

100 g / 4 oz unsalted butter
75 g / 3 oz icing sugar
25 g / 1 oz ground almonds
30 ml / 2 tbsp brandy
few drops of lemon juice

In a mixing bowl, cream the butter until very light. Sift in the icing sugar. a little at a time, and beat in each addition lightly but throughly with a fork. Add the almonds in the same way. Lift the fork when beating to incorporate as much air as possible. Beat in the brandy and lemon juice, a few drops at a time, taking care not to let the mixture separate. Taste, and add extra brandy if liked.

Pile the mixture into a dish and leave to firm up before serving; or turn lightly into a screwtopped jar and store in a cool place until required. Use within one week, or refrigerate for longer storage. Bring to room temperature before serving.

MAKES ABOUT 225 g / 8 oz

CHESTNUT BUTTER

200 g / 7 oz unsweetened chestnut purée
200 g / 7 oz butter, softened
30–45 ml / 2–3 tsp caster sugar
15–30 ml / 1–2 tbsp rum

Combine the chestnut purée and butter in a bowl and mix until thoroughly blended. Add the sugar and rum gradually, adjusting the flavour to taste. Chill until firm, then use at once, or pot and chill as for Orange Liqueur Butter (page 195).

MAKES ABOUT 450 g / 1 lb

Cakes & Baking

Christmas cake and its embellishments, Twelfth Night Cake, Stöllen, Bûche de Noel, Brandy Snaps, various mincemeats, mince pies, candied peel, decorative biscuits that make great gifts to hang on the tree – give your kitchen that holiday atmosphere!

CHRISTMAS CAKE

butter or oil for greasing
200 g / 7 oz plain flour
1.25 ml / ¼ tsp salt
5-10ml /1-2 tsp mixed spice
200 g / 7 oz butter
200 g/ 7 oz caster sugar
6 eggs, beaten
30–60 ml / 2–4 tbsp brandy or sherry
100 g / 4 oz glace cherries, chopped
50 g / 2 oz preserved ginger, chopped
50 g / 2 oz walnuts, chopped
200 g / 7 oz currants
200 g / 7 oz sultanas
150 g / 5 oz seedless raisins
75 g / 3 oz cut mixed peel

COATING AND ICING
Apricot Glaze (page 199)
Almond Paste (page 200)
Royal Icing (page 201)

Line and grease a 20-cm / 8-inch round cake tin. Use doubled greaseproof paper as a lining and tie a strip of brown paper around the outside. Set the oven at 160°C / 325°F / gas 3.

Stir the flour, salt and spice into a bowl. In a mixing bowl, cream the butter and sugar together until light and fluffy. Gradually beat in the eggs and the brandy or sherry, adding a little flour if the mixture starts to curdle. Add the cherries, ginger and walnuts. Stir in the dried fruit, peel and flour mixture. Spoon into the prepared tin and make a slight hollow in the centre.

Bake for 45 minutes then reduce the oven temperature to 150°C / 300°F / gas 2 and bake for a further hour. Reduce the temperature still further to 140°C / 275°F / gas 1, and continue cooking for 45–60 minutes until cooked though and firm to the touch. Cool in the tin. Cover the cake with Apricot Glaze (page 199), Almond Paste (page 200) and decorate with Royal Icing (page 201).

MAKES ONE 20-cm / 8-inch CAKE

MRS BEETON'S TIP

The quickest way to complete the decoration on a Christmas cake is to apply the royal icing in rough peaks, then add bought decoration. For a change, why not bake the cake mixture in a shaped tin, for example in the shape of a star or a bell. Shaped tins can be hired from kitchen shops and cake decorating suppliers.

To decide on the quantity of mixture which will fill an unusually-shaped tin, pour water into the tin until it is full to the brim. Measure the quantity of water as you are pouring it into the tin. Do the same with a 20-cm / 8-inch round tin. Compare the volumes and adjust the weight of ingredients accordingly.

APRICOT GLAZE

Brush this glaze over a cake before applying the marzipan. Any smooth yellow jam or marmalade may be used.

225 g / 8 oz apricot jam

Warm the jam with 30 ml / 2 tbsp water in a small saucepan over a low heat until the jam has melted. Sieve the mixture and return the glaze to the clean pan. Bring slowly to the boil allow to coot slightly before use.

SUFFICIENT TO COAT THE TOP AND SIDES OF ONE 20-cm / 8-inch CAKE

ALMOND PASTE

This recipe makes a pale, creamy yellow-coloured paste that can be used to cover and decorate cake, as well as for a base coat before applying icing.

225 g / 8 oz ground almonds
100 g / 4 oz caster sugar
100 g / 4 oz icing sugar
5 ml / 1 tsp lemon juice
few drops of almond essence
1 egg, beaten

Using a coarse sieve, sift the almonds, caster sugar and icing sugar into a mixing bowl. Add the lemon juice, almond essence and sufficient egg to bind the ingredients together. Knead lightly with the fingertips until smooth.

Wrap in cling film and overwrap in foil or a plastic bag to prevent the paste drying out. Store in a cool place until required.

MAKES ABOUT 450 g / 1 lb

MRS BEETON'S TIP

Don't knead the paste too much: this can draw the oils from the almonds and make the paste greasy. It will then be unsuitable as a base for icing.

ALMOND PASTE / MARZIPAN QUANTITIES

Quick guide to quantities required to cover cakes:

Round	**Quantity**
15 cm / 6 inches	350 g / 12 oz
18 cm / 7 inches	500 g / 18 oz

20 cm / 8 inches	575 g / 1¼ lb
23 cm / 9 inches	800 g / 1¾ lb
25 cm / 10 inches	900 g / 2 lb
28 cm / 11 inches	1 kg / 2¼ lb
30 cm / 12 inches	1.25 kg / 2¾ lb

Square	**Quantity**
15 cm / 6 inches	500 g / 18 oz
18 cm / 7 inches	575 g / 1¼ lb
20 cm / 8 inches	800 g / 1¾ lb
23 cm / 9 inches	900 g / 2 lb
25 cm / 10 inches	1 kg / 2¼ lb
28 cm / 11 inches	1.1 kg / 2½ lb
30 cm / 12 inches	1.4 kg / 3 lb

ROYAL ICING

It is vital to ensure that the bowl is clean and free from grease. Use a wooden spoon kept solely for the purpose and do not be tempted to skimp on the beating – insufficient beating will produce an off-white icing with a heavy, sticky texture.

2 egg whites
450 g / 1 lb icing sugar, sifted

Place the egg whites in a bowl and break them up with a fork. Gradually beat in about two-thirds of the icing sugar with a wooden spoon and continue beating for about 15 minutes until the icing is pure white and forms soft peaks. Add the remaining icing sugar, if necessary, to attain this texture. Cover the bowl with cling film and place a dampened tea-towel on top. Place the bowl inside a polythene bag if storing overnight or for longer.

Before use, lightly beat the icing to burst any air bubbles that have risen to the surface. Adjust the consistency for flat icing or piping.

SUFFICIENT TO COAT THE TOP AND SIDES OF ONE 20-cm / 8-inch CAKE

APPLYING ROYAL ICING

Royal icing cannot be applied directly to the bake because it would drag the crumbs and discolour badly, so rich fruit cakes are usually covered with a layer of almond paste or marzipan before the royal icing is applied. The secret of successful royal icing work, be it flat icing or piping, depends upon making the icing to the correct consistency.

ROYAL ICING QUANTITIES

Quick guide to quantities required to cover cakes (sufficient for 3 coats):

Round	**Quantity**
15 cm / 6 inch	575 g / 1¼ lb
18 cm / 7 inch	675 g / 1½ lb
20 cm / 8 inch	800 g / 1¾ lb
23 cm / 9 inch	900 g / 2 lb
25 cm / 10 inch	1 kg / 2¼ lb
28 cm / 11 inch	1.25 kg / 2¾ lb
30 cm / 12 inch	1.4 kg / 3 lb

Square	**Quantity**
15 cm / 6 inch	675 g / 1½ lb
18 cm / 7 inch	800 g / 1¾ lb
20 cm / 8 inch	900 g / 2 lb
23 cm / 9 inch	1 kg / 2¼ lb
25 cm / 10 inch	1.25 kg / 2¾ lb
28 cm / 11 inch	1.4 kg / 3 lb
30 cm / 12 inch	1.5 kg / 3¼ lb

MRS BEETON'S TIP

If the icing is to be used for a single cake, glycerine may be added to prevent it from becoming too brittle when dry. Add 2.5ml / ½ tsp glycerine during the final beating. Do not, however, use glycerine for a tiered cake where the icing must be hard in order to hold the tiers.

TWELFTH NIGHT CAKE

The tradition of the Twelfth Night Cake goes back to the days of the early Christian Church and beyond. In the Middle Ages, whoever found the bean in his cake became the 'Lord of Misrule' or 'King' for the festivities of Twelfth Night, with the finder of the pea as his 'Queen'. Finding the bean was thought to bring luck. The tradition survived until near the end of the nineteenth century.

margarine for greasing
150 g / 5 oz margarine
75 g / 3 oz soft dark brown sugar
3 eggs
300 g / 11 oz plain flour
60 ml / 4 tbsp milk
5 ml / 1 tsp bicarbonate of soda
30 ml / 2 tbsp golden syrup
2.5 ml / ½ tsp mixed spice
2.5 ml / ½ tsp ground cinnamon
pinch of salt
50 g / 2 oz currants
100 g / 4 oz sultanas
100 g / 4 oz cut mixed peel
1 dried bean (see above)
1 large dried whole pea (see above)

Line and grease a 15-cm / 6-inch round cake tin. Set the oven at 180°C / 350°F / gas 4. In a mixing bowl, cream the margarine and sugar until light and fluffy. Beat in the eggs, one at a time, adding a little flour with each. Warm the milk, add the bicarbonate of soda and stir until dissolved. Add the syrup.

Mix the spices and salt with the remaining flour in a bowl. Add this to the creamed mixture alternately with the flavoured milk. Lightly stir the dried fruit and peel. Spoon half the cake mixture into the prepared tin, lay the bean and pea in the centre, then cover with the rest of the cake mixture. Bake for about 2 hours. Cool on a wire rack.

MAKES ONE 15-cm / 6-inch CAKE

CHRISTMAS STÖLLEN

This is the classic German Christmas bread.

butter for greasing
1 kg / 2¼ lb plain flour
75 g / 3 oz fresh yeast
200 ml / 7 fl oz lukewarm milk
350 g / 12 oz butter
grated rind and juice of 1 lemon
250 g / 9 oz caster sugar
2 egg yolks
5 ml / 1 tsp salt
500 g / 18 oz seedless raisins
225 g / 8 oz sultanas
150 g / 5 oz blanched slivered almonds
100 g / 4 oz chopped mixed peel
flour for dusting
100 g / 4 oz unsalted butter
icing sugar for dusting

Butter a baking sheet. Sift the flour into a bowl. Blend the yeast with the warm milk and 50 g / 2 oz of the flour. Set aside until frothy.

Meanwhile, melt the butter. Cool slightly, then blend into the remaining flour with the lemon juice. Add the milk and yeast liquid together with the lemon rind, sugar, egg yolks and salt. Beat well together. Knead the dough until it is very firm and elastic, and leaves the sides of the bowl. Cover with cling film. Leave in a warm place until the dough has doubled in bulk. This will take about 2 hours.

Meanwhile, mix the dried fruit with the nuts and mixed peel. Knead the dough again, pull the sides to the centre, turn it over and cover once more. Leave to rise for a further 30 minutes. When the dough has doubled in bulk again, turn it on to a floured surface and knead in the fruit and nut mixture.

Divide the dough in half and roll each half into a pointed oval shape. Lay each on the prepared baking sheet. Place a rolling pin along the length of each piece of the dough in the centre. Roll half the dough lightly from the centre outwards.

Brush the thinner rolled half with a little water and fold the other half over it, leaving a margin of about 5 cm / 2 inches all around which allows the dough to rise. Press well together; the water will bind it. Cover the stöllen and leave to rise in a warm place until doubled in bulk again. Set the oven at 190ºC / 375ºF / gas 5.

Melt 50 g / 2 oz of the unsalted butter and brush it over the stöllen. Bake for about 1 hour, until golden. When baked, melt the remaining unsalted butter, brush it over the stöllen, then sprinkle with sifted icing sugar. Keep for a day before cutting.

The stöllen will remain fresh for many weeks if well wrapped in foil or greaseproof paper and stored in an airtight tin.

MAKES TWO LOAVES,
ABOUT 24 SLICES EACH

BÛCHE DE NÖEL (CHESTNUT CHRISTMAS LOG)

SPONGE

butter for greasing
100 g / 4 oz icing sugar
3 eggs
4 tsp rum
65 g / 2½ oz self-raising flour
icing sugar for dusting

FILLING

2 x 440 g / 15 oz cans unsweetened chestnut purée
275 g / 10 oz butter, softened
125 g / 4½ oz caster sugar
2 tbsp rum

DECORATION

marrons glacés or glacé cherries and angelica

Grease a 35 x 25-cm / 14 x 10-inch Swiss roll tin and line it with greased paper. Set the oven at 220°C / 425°F / gas 7.

Warm a mixing bowl with hot water, then dry it. Sift the icing sugar into the bowl and break in the eggs. Beat or whisk vigorously for 5–10 minutes until the mixture is very light and fluffy, adding the rum while beating. When the mixture is like meringue, fold in the flour gently. Turn the mixture into the prepared tin and bake for 7 minutes. Meanwhile, prepare a 40 x 30-cm / 16 x 12-inch sheet of greaseproof paper, beginning at one long side to make a long thin roll, or at one short end for a shorter roll. Cool.

Meanwhile, prepare the chestnut butter cream for the filling. Turn the purée into a bowl and beat in the butter, then add the sugar and rum.

When the sponge is cold, unroll it carefully. Cover the underside of the sponge with just over half the butter cream, laying it on thickly at the further edge. Then re-roll the sponge, and place it on a sheet of greaseproof paper, with the cut edge underneath. Cover the sponge with the remaining butter cream, either spreading with a knife or using a piping bag with a ribbon nozzle, and imitating the knots and grain of wood. Chill and serve decorated with glazed chestnuts or fruit.

SERVES SIX TO EIGHT

APPLE AND GINGER CAKE

butter or margarine for greasing
175 g / 6 oz plain flour
1.25 ml / ¼ tsp salt
2.5 ml / ½ tsp bicarbonate of soda
5 ml / 1 tsp baking powder
5 ml / 1 tsp ground ginger
100 g / 4 oz crystallized ginger, chopped
100 g / 4 oz butter or margarine
150 g / 5 oz caster sugar
2 eggs, beaten
250 ml / 9 fl oz sieved apple purée

Line and grease an 18-cm / 7-inch square tin. Set the oven at 180°C / 350°F / gas 4. Sift the flour, salt, bicarbonate of soda, baking powder and ground ginger into a bowl. Stir in the crystallized ginger and mix well. Set aside.

Place the butter or margarine in a mixing bowl and beat until very soft. Add the sugar and cream together until light and fluffy. Add the beaten eggs gradually, beating well after each addition. If the mixture shows signs of curdling, add a little of the flour mixture. Stir in the apple purée. Fold in the dry ingredients lightly but thoroughly. Spoon into the prepared tin, smooth the surface and make a slight hollow in the centre.

Bake for 30 minutes, then reduce the oven temperature to 160°C / 325°F / gas 3 and bake for 15 minutes more until firm to the touch. Cool on a wire rack.

MAKES ONE 18-cm / 7-inch CAKE

BLACK FOREST GÂTEAU

butter or margarine for greasing
150 g / 5 oz butter or margarine
150 g / 5 oz caster sugar
3 eggs, beaten
few drops of vanilla essence
100 g / 4 oz self-raising flour or plain flour
and 5 ml / 1 tsp baking powder
25 g / 1 oz cocoa
pinch of salt

FILLING AND TOPPING
250 ml / 9 fl oz double cream
125 ml / 4 fl oz single cream
1 x 540 g / 19 oz can Morello cherries
kirsch (see method)
25 g / 1 oz plain chocolate, grated

Line and grease a 20-cm / 8-inch cake tin. Set the oven at 180°C / 350°F / gas 4.

In a mixing bowl, cream the butter or margarine with the sugar until light and fluffy. Add the eggs gradually, beating well after each addition. Stir in the vanilla essence.

Sift the flour, cocoa, salt and baking powder, if used, into a bowl. Stir into the creamed mixture, lightly but thoroughly, until evenly mixed.

Spoon into the tin and bake for 40 minutes. Cool on a wire rack. When quite cold, carefully cut the cake into three layers, brushing all loose crumbs off the cut sides.

Make the filling. Combine the creams in a bowl and whip until stiff. Place half the whipped cream in another bowl.

Drain the cherries, reserving the juice. Set aside 11 whole cherries and halve and stone the remainder. Gently fold the halved cherries into one of the bowls of cream. Set aside. Strain the reserved cherry juice into a measuring jug and add kirsch to taste.

Prick the cake layers and sprinkle with the cherry juice and kirsch until well saturated. Sandwich the layers together with the whipped cream and cherries. When assembled, cover with the remaining plain cream and use the whole cherries to decorate the top. Sprinkle the grated chocolate over the cream.

SERVES TEN TO TWELVE

RICH GINGERBREAD

butter for greasing
225 g / 8 oz plain flour
1.25 ml / ¼ tsp salt
10 ml / 2 tsp ground ginger
2.5–5 ml / ½–1 tsp ground cinnamon or grated nutmeg
5 ml / 1 tsp bicarbonate of soda
100 g / 4 oz butter
100 g / 4 oz soft light brown sugar
100 g / 4 oz golden syrup
1 egg
45 ml / 3 tbsp plain yogurt
30 ml / 2 tbsp ginger preserve

Line and grease a 20-cm / 8-inch square baking tin. Set the oven at 160°C / 325°F / gas 3.

Sift the flour, salt, spices and bicarbonate of soda into a mixing bowl. Heat the butter, sugar and syrup gently in a saucepan until the butter has melted.

In a bowl, beat the egg and yogurt together. Add to the dry ingredients, with the melted mixture, to give a soft, dropping consistency. Stir in the preserve.

Spoon into the prepared tin and bake for 50-60 minutes until cooked through and firm to the touch. Cool on a wire rack.

MAKES ONE 23-cm / 9-inch CAKE

CINNAMON BARS

butter for greasing
175 g / 6 oz plain flour
5 ml / 1 tsp ground cinnamon
50 g / 2 oz caster sugar
100 g / 4 oz butter
25 g / 1 oz flaked almonds
15 ml / 1 tbsp granulated sugar

Grease a 30 x 20-cm / 12 x 8-inch Swiss roll tin. Set the oven at 180°C / 350°F / gas 4.

Sift the flour and 2.5 ml / ½ tsp of the cinnamon into a mixing bowl and add the caster sugar. Rub in the butter until the mixture resembles firm breadcrumbs and work into a soft dough. Press the mixture into the prepared tin. Flatten and level the surface, then sprinkle with the flaked almonds, granulated sugar and remaining cinnamon.

Bake for 15–20 minutes in the preheated oven until golden brown. Cut into bars or fingers while still warm.

MAKES ABOUT TWENTY

MRS BEETON'S TIP

For a look that children will love, substitute coloured sugar granules (sometimes called coffee sugar) for the granulated sugar in the topping. Omit the cinnamon.

FLORENTINES

oil for greasing
25 g / 1 oz glacé cherries, chopped
100 g / 4 oz cut mixed peel, finely chopped
50 g / 2 oz flaked almonds
100 g / 4 oz chopped almonds
25 g / 1 oz sultanas
100 g / 4 oz butter or margarine
100 g / 4 oz caster sugar
30 ml / 2 tbsp double cream
100 g / 4 oz plain or courverture chocolate

Line three or four baking sheets with oiled greaseproof paper. Set the oven at 180°C / 350°F / gas 4.

In a bowl, mix the cherries and mixed peel with the flaked and chopped almonds and the sultanas. Melt the butter or margarine in a small saucepan, add the sugar and boil for 1 minute. Remove from the heat and stir in the fruit and nuts. Whip the cream in a separate bowl, then fold it in.

Place small spoonfuls of the mixture on to the prepared baking sheets, leaving room for spreading. Bake for 8-10 minutes. After the biscuits have been cooking for about 5 minutes, neaten the edges by drawing them together with the plain biscuit cutter. Leave the cooked biscuits on the baking sheets to firm up slightly before transferring to a wire rack to cool completely.

To finish, melt the chocolate in a bowl set over a pan of hot water and use to coat the flat underside of each biscuit. Mark into wavy lines with a fork as the chocolate cools.

MAKES TWENTY TO TWENTY FOUR

BRANDY SNAPS

These traditional treats make a popular addition to a buffet table or may be served as a tempting dessert. Fill them at the last moment with fresh whipped cream.

butter or margarine for greasing
50 g / 2 oz plain flour
5 ml / 1 tsp ground ginger
50 g / 2 oz butter or margarine
50 g / 2 oz soft dark brown sugar
30 ml / 2 tbsp golden syrup
10 ml / 2 tsp grated lemon rind
5 ml / 1 tsp lemon juice

Grease two or three 25 x 20-cm / 10 x 8-inch baking sheets. Also grease the handles of several wooden spoons, standing them upside down in a jar until required. Set the oven at 180°C / 350°F / gas 4.

Sift the flour and ginger into a bowl. Melt the butter or margarine in a saucepan. Add the sugar and syrup and warm gently, but do not allow to become hot. Remove from the heat and add the sifted ingredients with the lemon rind and juice. Mix well.

Put spoonfuls of the mixture on the prepared baking sheets spacing well apart to allow for spreading. Do not put more than 6 spoonfuls on a baking sheet. Bake for 8–10 minutes.

Remove from the oven and leave to cool for a few seconds until the edges begin to firm. Lift one of the biscuits with a palette knife and roll loosely around the greased handle of one of the wooden spoons. Allow to cool before removing biscuits. Alternatively, make brandy snap cups by moulding the mixture in greased patty tins or over oranges.

MAKES FOURTEEN TO EIGHTEEN

GERMAN SPICE BISCUITS

butter or margarine for greasing
100 g / 4 oz plain flour
50 g / 2 oz caster sugar
1.25 ml / ¼ tsp mixed spice
75 g / 3 oz butter or margarine
flour for rolling out

Grease a baking sheet. Set the oven at 160°C / 325°F / gas 3.

Mix the flour, sugar and spice in a mixing bowl. Rub in the butter or margarine until the mixture binds together and forms a pliable dough.

Roll out on a floured board to a thickness of 5 mm / ¼ inch and cut into rounds with a 6-cm / 2½-inch round cutter. Place on the prepared baking sheet. Bake for about 20 minutes until very pale gold in colour. Leave to stand for a few minutes, then cool on a wire rack.

MAKES ABOUT TWELVE

MRS BEETON'S TIP

A glass makes a good biscuit cutter. Dip it in flour before use to prevent the dough from sticking to the rim.

CHOCOLATE-TIPPED CINNAMON STARS

butter for greasing
350 g / 12 oz plain flour
5 ml / 1 tsp bicarbonate of soda
10 ml / 2 tsp ground cinnamon
2.5 ml / ½ tsp ground ginger
150 g / 5 oz butter
100 g / 4 oz sugar
100 g / 4 oz honey
1 egg yolk
30 ml / 2 tbsp milk
flour for rolling out
150 g / 5 oz plain chocolate, broken into squares, to decorate

Thoroughly grease three or four baking sheets. Set the oven at 180°C / 350°F / gas 4. Mix the flour, bicarbonate of soda and spices in a bowl.

In another bowl, beat the butter until soft, add the sugar and continue to beat until light and fluffy. Beat in the honey and egg yolk, then the milk. Fold in the flour mixture.

Knead the biscuit dough lightly on a floured surface, then roll out to a thickness of 3 mm / ⅛ inch. Cut into stars with a 5-cm / 2-inch star-shaped biscuit cutter. Using a straw, make a small hole in each star. The hole should be on a point, but not too near the edge. Transfer the biscuits to the prepared baking sheets.

Bake for about 8 minutes, until golden brown. Cool for a few minutes on the baking sheets then transfer to wire racks.

Melt the chocolate with 15 ml / 1 tbsp water in a saucepan over low heat. Brush the tips of each star generously with chocolate, then place on a wire rack until the chocolate has set. When the chocolate is firm, thread a length of ribbon through each biscuit and hand on the Christmas tree.

MAKES ABOUT 60

MINCE PIES

Festive mince pies can also be made using Flaky (page 221), Rough Puff (page 222) or Puff Pastry (page 74) with mouthwatering results. If using any of these pastries you will require 200 g / 7 oz flour.

350 g / 12 oz Mincemeat (pages 218–220)
25 g / 1 oz icing or caster sugar for dredging

SHORT CRUST PASTRY
300 g / 11 oz plain flour
5 ml / 1 tsp salt
150 g / 5 oz margarine (or half butter, half lard)
flour for rolling out

Set the oven at 200°C / 400°F / gas 6. To make the pastry, soft the flour and salt into a bowl, then rub in the margarine until the mixture resembles fine breadcrumbs. Add enough cold water to make a stiff dough. Press the dough together with your fingertips.

Roll out the pastry on a lightly floured surface and use just over half of it to line twelve 7.5-cm / 3-inch patty tins. Cut out 12 lids from the rest of the pastry. If liked, make holly leaf decorations from the pastry trimmings.

Place a spoonful of mincemeat in each pastry case. Dampen the edges of the cases and cover with the pastry lids. Seal the edges well. Brush the tops with water and add any pastry decorations. Dredge with the sugar. Make 2 small cuts in the top of each pie. Bake for 15–20 minutes or until golden brown.

MAKES TWELVE

MINCEMEAT MERINGUE PIE

50 g / 2 oz soft white breadcrumbs
30 ml / 2 tbsp granulated sugar
2 eggs, separated
375 ml / 13 fl oz milk
15 ml / 1 tbsp butter
2.5 ml / ½ tsp vanilla essence
225 g / 8 oz mincemeat
75 g / 3 oz caster sugar

SHORT CRUST PASTRY
100 g / 4 oz plain flour
2.5 ml / ½ tsp salt
50 g / 2 oz margarine (or half butter, half lard)
flour for rolling out

Set the oven at 200°C / 400°F / gas 6. To make the pastry, sift the flour and salt into a bowl, then rub in the margarine until the mixture resembles fine breadcrumbs. Add enough cold water to make a stiff dough. Press the dough together with your fingertips.

Roll out the pastry on a lightly floured surface and use to line an 18-cm / 7-inch flan tin or ring placed on a baking sheet. Line the pastry with greaseproof paper and fill with baking beans. Bake 'blind' for 10 minutes, then remove the paper and beans. Return to the oven for 5 minutes, then remove. Lower the oven temperature to 180°C / 350°F / gas 4.

Combine the breadcrumbs, sugar and egg yolks in a bowl and mix well. Warm the milk and butter together in a saucepan until the butter has just melted, then stir slowly into the breadcrumb mixture. Mix well, then stir in the vanilla essence. Leave to stand for 5 minutes.

Pour the breadcrumb filling into the flan case and bake for 35–45 minutes or until the custard is firm. Remove from the oven.

Raise the oven temperature to 200°C / 400°F / gas 6. Spread the mincemeat over the crumb custard. Whisk the egg whites in a clean, grease-free bowl until stiff, gradually whisking in about 50 g / 2 oz of the caster sugar. Pile or spoon the meringue over the pie filling, covering both the mincemeat and the pastry edge completely. Sprinkle with the remaining sugar. Bake for 5–10 minutes until the meringue is golden. Serve at once, with single cream.

SERVES FOUR TO SIX

CRANBERRY RAISIN PIE

225 g / 8 oz cranberries
175 g / 6 oz raisins
150 g / 5 oz sugar
30 ml / 2 tbsp plain flour
1.25 ml / ¼ tsp salt
25 g / 1 oz butter, diced

SHORT CRUST PASTRY
225 g / 8 oz plain flour
2.5 ml / ½ tsp salt
100 g / 4 oz margarine (or half butter, half lard)
flour for rolling out

Set the oven at 200°C / 400°F / gas 6. To make the pastry, sift the flour and salt into a bowl, then rub in the margarine until the mixture resembles fine breadcrumbs. Add enough cold water to make a stiff dough. Press the dough together with your fingertips. Roll out on a lightly floured surface and use two-thirds of the pastry to line a 23-cm / 9-inch pie plate.

In a bowl, combine the cranberries and raisins with the sugar, flour and salt. Mix lightly, then spoon into the pastry case. Dot with the butter.

Roll out the remaining pastry into a rectangle and cut into five 1 cm / ½ inch strips. Arrange the strips in a lattice on top of the pie. Bake for 10 minutes, then reduce the oven temperature to 180°C / 350°F / gas 4 and bake for 30–40 minutes more.

SERVES SIX

EXCELLENT MINCEMEAT

3 large cooking apples, cored
3 large lemons
450 g / 1 lb raisins
450 g / 1 lb currants
450 g / 1 lb suet
900 g / 2 lb soft light brown sugar
25 g / 1 oz candied orange peel, chopped
25 g / 1 oz candied citron or lemon peel, chopped
30 ml / 2 tbsp orange marmalade
250 ml / 9 fl oz brandy

Set the oven at 200°C / 400°F / gas 6. Place the cooking apples in an ovenproof dish, cover tightly and bake for 50–60 minutes, until thoroughly tender. Leave to cool.

Wash, dry and grate the lemons. Squeeze out the juice and reserve with the rind. Chop the shells, place them in a small saucepan and add cold water to cover. Bring to the boil, lower the heat and cover the pan. Simmer for about 1 hour, or until the shells are soft enough to chop very finely. Drain, cool and chop.

Scoop the apple flesh from the skins. Place it in a large bowl. Stir in the reserved lemon rind and juice with all the remaining ingredients. Cover the bowl and leave for 2 days, stirring occasionally. Pot, pressing the mincemeat down well. Cover tightly and store for at least 2 weeks before using.

MAKES ABOUT 4 kg / 9 lb

LEMON MINCEMEAT

2 large lemons
900 g / 2 lb cooking apples, peeled, cored and minced
225 g / 8 oz shredded suet
450 g / 1 lb currants
225 g / 8 oz sugar
75 g / 3 oz candied citron and lemon or orange peel, chopped
10 ml / 2 tsp ground mixed spice

Wash, dry and pare the lemons thinly, avoiding the pith. Place the rind in a small saucepan with water to cover. Bring to the boil, lower the heat and simmer for 15 minutes, or until the rind is tender. Drain and chop the rind. Squeeze the lemons and put the juice in a mixing bowl.

Add the apples to the bowl along with the lemon rind, suet, currants, sugar, candied peel and spice. Stir well, cover tightly and leave for 1 week, stirring occasionally.

The mincemeat will be ready to use at the end of the week; however, it may be potted or put in containers, covered tightly and stored in a cool place for a further 2–3 weeks. It will also freeze well.

MAKES ABOUT 2.25 kg / 5 lb

VEGETARIAN MINCEMEAT

200 g / 7 oz raisins
100 g / 4 oz sultanas
100 g / 4 oz currants
100 g / 4 oz dried apricots, chopped
100 g / 4 oz cut mixed peel, chopped
45 ml / 3 tbsp honey
60 ml / 4 tbsp brandy
2.5 ml / ½ tsp each ground cinnamon, grated nutmeg and salt
200 g / 7 oz thick apple purée, fresh or canned
grated rind of 1 lemon
grated rind of 1 orange

Combine the dried fruits and peel. Put the remaining ingredients into a small saucepan and bring to the boil slowly. Stir the mixture and pour over the fruits. Mix well and leave to cool.

Pot in sterilised jars, cover with waxed discs and screw-on lids, and label. Store in a cool, dry place for up to three weeks, or in the refrigerator for up to four weeks.

MAKES ABOUT 1 kg / 2¼ lb

QUICK CANDIED PEEL

Soak grapefruit or lemon peel overnight to extract some of the bitterness. Cut the peel into long strips, 5-mm / ¼-inch wide. Put in a saucepan, cover with cold water and bring slowly to the boil. Drain, add fresh water and bring to the boil again. Drain, and repeat 3 more times. Weigh the cooled peel and place with an equal quantity of sugar in a pan. Just cover with boiling water, and boil gently until the peel is tender and clear. Cool, strain from the syrup, and toss the peel in caster or granulated sugar on greaseproof paper. Spread out on a wire rack to dry for several hours. Roll again in sugar if at all sticky. When quite dry, store in covered jars. Use within 3–4 months.

FLAKY PASTRY

Flaky pastry does not have as many layers as puff pastry. It contains less fat to flour and the dough is rolled and folded fewer times.

225 g / 8 oz plain flour
1.25 ml / ¼ tsp salt
175 g / 6 oz butter or 75 g / 3 oz each butter and lard, chilled
5 ml / 1 tsp lemon juice
flour for rolling out

Sift the flour and salt into a bowl. If using butter and lard, roughly mix them together. Rub in a quarter of the fat, keeping the remaining fat chilled. Stir in the lemon juice and enough cold water to mix the ingredients to a soft dough. The mixture should take about 125 ml / 4 fl oz water but this should be added by the spoonful to avoid making the dough too wet.

On a lightly floured surface, roll out the dough into an oblong measuring about 25 x 15 cm / 10 x 6 inches. Mark the dough into thirds. Cut the fat into 3 equal portions. Dot a portion of fat over the top two-thirds of the dough, in neat lumps.

Fold the bottom third of the dough up over the middle portion, then fold the top third down so that the lumps of fat are enclosed completely. Press the edges of the dough together with the rolling pin. Give the dough a quarter turn clockwise, then roll out as before.

Repeat the process of dotting the dough with fat, folding and rolling it, twice more. Chill the dough briefly between each rolling. Finally, fold and roll the pastry once more, without any fat, then chill again before using it as required.

MAKES ABOUT 450 g / 1 lb

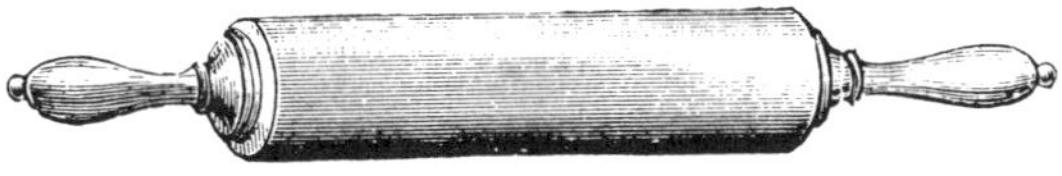

ROUGH PUFF PASTRY

A slightly easier version of puff pastry; all the fat must be well chilled for success. For best results, chill the bowl of flour too; always make sure your hands are very cold by holding them under cold running water before handling the dough.

225 g / 8 oz plain flour
1.25 ml / ¼ tsp salt
175 g / 6 oz butter, cut in chunks and chilled
5 ml / 1 tsp lemon juice
flour for rolling out

Sift the flour and salt into a bowl. Add the butter and mix in lightly using a round-bladed knife. Mix in the lemon juice and enough ice-cold water to make a soft dough. The mixture should take about 125 ml / 4 fl oz (or very slightly more) but add the water a spoonful at a time to avoid making the dough too wet. The dough should be soft and very lumpy.

On a lightly floured surface roll out the dough into an oblong, keeping the corners square. Mark the oblong of dough into thirds, then fold and roll it as for Flaky Pastry (page 221). Repeat the process four times in all, chilling the dough between each rolling or as necessary.

The rolled dough should be smooth. Wrap it in cling film and chill well before rolling it out to use as required.

MAKES ABOUT 450 g / 1 lb

TIPS FOR SUCCESS WITH PASTRY

- Work in a cool place; keep hands, utensils and all ingredients cool.
- Weigh and measure all ingredients accurately.
- Handle pastry as lightly as possible, and work as quickly as you can, at all stages.
- Use the minimum amount of flour for rolling out.
- Chill short crust, flaky and puff pastry for 20–30 minutes before rolling out.
- Chill short crust, puff or flaky pastry goods for 15 minutes before baking.

Beverages

Specially-made drinks really add sparkle to celebrations. Make alcohol-free punch for drivers, teetotallers and children, and add Christmas spice by mulling wine, ale or cider. Port-based, traditional Bishop will really get the party going!

ALCOHOL-FREE PUNCH

300 g / 11 oz caster sugar
150 ml / ¼ pint strong black tea
250 ml / 9 fl oz lemon juice
350 ml / 12 fl oz orange juice
1 litre / 1¾ pints white grape juice
1 x 227 g / 8 oz can crushed pineapple
2 litres / 3½ pints ginger ale
ice cubes
1 x 170 g / 6 oz bottle maraschino cherries, drained
2 lemons, sliced
2 oranges, sliced

Put the sugar in a large saucepan with 3.5 litres / 6 pints water. Stir over gentle heat until the sugar has dissolved, then boil for 6 minutes. Stir in the tea and set aside until cool. Pour into one or two large jugs or bowls; cover and chill.

When quite cold, add the fruit juices and crushed pineapple. Just before serving, pour in the ginger ale and add the ice cubes. Add the maraschino cherries, stir once and serve with the citrus slices floating on top.

SERVES ABOUT 48

MULLED WINE

This traditional Christmas drink used to be heated by means of a red-hot mulling poker. Today the mixture is more likely to be made on top of the stove, but it remains a welcome warmer on a cold winter's night.

100 g / 4 oz caster sugar
4 cinnamon sticks
4 cloves
1 nutmeg
2 oranges, thinly sliced
1 bottle red wine

Boil 600 ml / 1 pint water with the sugar and spices in a saucepan for 5 minutes. Add the oranges, remove the pan from the hear and set aside for 15 minutes.

Stir in the wine. Heat slowly without boiling. Serve very hot, in heated glasses.

SERVES EIGHT

MULLED ALE

1 litre / 1¾ pints ale
15–30 ml / 1–2 tbsp caster sugar
generous pinch of ground cloves
pinch of grated nutmeg
generous pinch of ground ginger
100 ml / 3½ fl oz rum or brandy

Combine the ale, 15 ml / 1 tbsp caster sugar and the spices in a large saucepan. Bring to just below boiling point. Remove from the heat and stir in the rum or brandy, with more sugar if required. Ladle into heated glasses and serve at once.

SERVES EIGHT

MULLED CIDER

1.2 litres / 2 pints cider
1.2 litres / 2 pints red grape juice
450 ml / 16 fl oz orange juice
230 ml / 8 fl oz brandy
3 lemons, sliced
3 oranges, sliced
2 pieces candied ginger
1 stick cinnamon
4 whole cloves
2 cardamom pods

Put the cider, juices, lemons, and oranges in a large saucepan. Tie ginger and spices in a muslin bag, add to saucepan. Bring to the boil the reduce heat. Simmer, uncovered for fifteen minutes. Remove spice bag and add the brandy. Serve warm in a punch bowl.

SERVES TEN TO TWELVE

BISHOP

12 cloves
1 large orange
1 x 700 ml / 24 fl oz bottle of port
granulated sugar

Press the cloves into the orange and put it in an ovenproof bowl. Cover tightly with foil. Set the oven at 180°C / 350°F / gas 4. Roast the orange until lightly browned. Cut into eight pieces and remove the pips.

Pour the port into an enamel or stainless steel saucepan, add the pieces of orange and heat gently to simmering point. Sweeten to taste with sugar and simmer gently for 20 minutes, taking care not to let the liquor boil. Strain through a fine sieve immediately and serve.

FILLS TWELVE SHERRY GLASSES

FRUIT CLARET CUP

This is a good basic fruit cup. The proportions of claret and soda water may be altered to suit personal taste.

cracked ice
50 ml / 2 fl oz brandy
30 ml / 2 tbsp caster sugar
30 ml / 2 tbsp maraschino liqueur
6 maraschino cherries
30 ml / 2 tbsp lemon juice
1 lemon, sliced and quartered
1 orange, sliced and quartered
6 thin slices of fresh pineapple, quartered
1 litre / 1¾ pints claret
175 ml / 6 fl oz soda water

Put some cracked ice into a large jug. Add the brandy, sugar, maraschino liqueur and cherries. Strain in the lemon juice and add the fresh fruit. Stir in the claret.

Just before serving, add the soda water and stir once.

SERVES TWELVE

VARIATIONS

- **Curaçao and Claret Cup** Substitute curaçao for the brandy. Increase the quantity of maraschino to 40 ml / 1½ fl oz. Omit the lemon and pineapple. When serving the cup, add 1 sliced red apple.
- **Claret and Lemonade Cooler** Pour the claret on to cracked ice in a large bowl or jug. Strain in 450 ml / 16 fl oz lemon juice. Add 1 litre / 1¾ pints lemonade or soda water just before serving.

WHISKY PUNCH

thinly pared rind and juice of 3 lemons
1 litre / 1¾ pints boiling water
1 x 700 ml / 24 fl oz bottle blended whisky
200 g / 7 oz lump sugar

Strain the lemon juice and put it in a bowl with the lemon rind. Pour the boiling water over it, then add the whisky and stir in the sugar. When the sugar has dissolved, strain the liquid and serve at once.

FILLS FIFTEEN WINE GLASSES

RUM AND BRANDY TODDY

225 g / 8 oz sugar lumps
2 large lemons, washed
600 ml / 1 pint rum
600 ml / 1 pint brandy
5 ml / 1 tsp grated nutmeg

Rub a few of the sugar lumps over the lemon to absorb the oil. Put them in a heatproof bowl with the remaining sugar lumps. Squeeze the lemons and strain the juice into the bowl, then crush the sugar with a wooden spoon.

Pour 1.1 litres / 2 pints boiling water into the bowl, stir well, then add the remaining ingredients. Mix thoroughly. Serve at once.

SERVES EIGHT TO TEN

ORANGE BRANDY

For the best flavour, use Seville oranges.

175 g / 6 oz sugar lumps
2 oranges, washed
1 x 700 ml / 24 fl oz bottle of brandy

Rub a few of the sugar lumps over the oranges to absorb the oil. Put them in a large bowl with the remaining sugar lumps.

Pare the orange peel in thin strips, taking care to avoid the pith, and add to the bowl. Squeeze the oranges and strain the juice into the bowl. Crush the sugar cubes with a spoon. Stir in the brandy. Pour into a large jar, close tightly and set aside for 3 days, stirring several times a day.

When all the sugar has dissolved, strain the mixture into clean bottles. Cork tightly and store in a cool, dry place. The flavour will improve on keeping, and the brandy should ideally be stored for 1 year before being opened.

MAKES ABOUT 1 litre / 1¾ pints

HOME-MADE NOYEAU

This nut-flavoured liqueur can be used to flavour puddings and cakes.

150 ml / ¼ pint milk
100 g / 4 oz whole unblanched almonds
15 ml / 1 tbsp liquid honey
225 g / 8 oz caster sugar
grated rind of 1 lemon
1 x 700 ml / 24 fl oz bottle Irish whiskey
150 ml / ¼ pint single cream

Combine the milk, almonds and honey in a saucepan. Bring to the boil, remove from the heat, cover and leave to stand until quite cold.

Strain the milk into a jug. Grind the almonds in a nut mill or food processor, or pound in a mortar with a pestle.

Transfer the ground almonds to a bowl and stir in the sugar. Add the lemon rind and whiskey, then stir in the cold milk and honey mixture. Add the cream. Pour into a large jar, close tightly and store for 10 days, shaking daily.

Pour the mixture through a filter paper into a large jug. Fill small bottles, corking them tightly. Store in a cool, dry place.

MAKES ABOUT 900 ml / 1½ pints

Table Laying, Menu Planning & Christmas Countdown

TABLE LAYING

Following dining trends, there are many options for table laying, from formal settings to casual, yet attractive presentations.

PLACE SETTINGS

If soup is to be served, round soup spoons or dessert spoons should be provided. Special fish knives and forks can be laid for the fish course; the knives are blunt with a slightly pointed end which enables the bones to be eased out of the fish without cutting the flesh. Large knives and forks are laid for the main meat course, with a small knife for bread and butter and cheese. Steak knives with a serrated cutting edge are often used for grilled steak or chops. A dessertspoon and fork are provided for the sweet course, or a teaspoon if the dessert is to be served in small dishes or glasses. If fresh fruit is being served, the appropriate knives and forks should be provided.

TABLE DECORATIONS

Flower arrangements should be low and flowers must not be overpoweringly scented. Candles should match table linen and/or room decor. Wine should be placed ready on the sideboard or side table together with a jug of iced water and soft drinks. Sauceboats should have a stand or saucer to avoid drips on the tablecloth.

THE BUFFET TABLE

The art of laying a buffet table is to show off the food to its best advantage while making serving easy.

For buffets to serve 50 people or more, place plates and cutlery at either end of the buffet table so that there at least two serving points. This means that there must be two platters (at least) of each dish so that guests may help themselves from either end of the table. Drinks, and later coffee, should be served from a side table. Depending on the space available, the dessert can be displayed ready on a side table, or served from the main table when the main course is finished. Use cake stands for gateau-type desserts to vary the height of the display. The most convenient way to lay cutlery is to wrap a set for each person in a table napkin. Distribute cruets along the table, and accompaniments (salad dressing or sauce) near the appropriate dishes. Place bread or rolls with butter at each end of the table. Cheeseboards should be brought in with the dessert and placed at each end of the buffet with celery, biscuits and butter, and, of course, small plates and knives. For small buffets, it is usually possible to lay everything on one table with cutlery and plates at one end only.

TRADITIONAL FORMAL SETTINGS

Lay the knives, blades pointing inwards, on the right of the dinner plate and the forks on the left in the order in which they will be used (first to be used on the extreme right or left and the last next to the plate). The dessertspoon and fork can either be laid in neat alignment across the top of the setting, with the spoon handle to the right and the fork handle to the left, or at the sides of the plate, spoon on the right, fork on the left; either arrangement is correct. Fruit knives and forks can be laid across the top of the setting with the dessertspoon and fork, or at the side. Alternatively, they can be handed round with the dessert plates. The small knife for bread may go next to the dinner plate, on the right-hand side or vertically across the side plate, which should be on the left of the place setting. The soup spoon is placed on the extreme right-hand side as this is the first implement to be used. Line up the cutlery neatly and as closely together as is practical, with the handles about 1 cm / ½ inch from the edge of the table.

Glasses should be arranged in a straight line across the top of the right-hand cutlery, in the order of use; for example, a glass for white wine on the right, then one for red, and a port or liqueur glass on the left of the row. If you include a tumbler or stemmed glass for water, place this before the liqueur glass. The last glass should be placed just above the meat knife. If you are laying a single wine glass, put it anywhere above the right-hand cutlery.

Finger-bowls, if used, are placed to the left just above the line of forks. Table napkins can be put in the centre of the place setting, on the side plate or in one of the glasses.

ALTERNATIVE SETTINGS

A completely different approach to table laying is sometimes suitable for casual or everyday entertaining. Place mats are widely used instead of tablecloths, on both formal and casual occasions. The table setting may be changed completely to reflect the food as when Chinese bowls, chopsticks, spoons and forks replace the traditional cutlery. For an informal, one-course meal, the cutlery (usually a knife and fork) may be placed neatly together on a napkin on the side plate in the centre of the setting. Match bright china with colourful napkins, flowers or ribbons to emphasize the light-hearted approach.

CUTLERY AND CONDIMENTS

Whatever the type of meal, always make sure the necessary serving utensils are on the table.

Traditionally, serving spoons and forks are paired at both ends of the table, according to the number of dishes, arranged as for the dessert cutlery. Have all the implements for serving the main course on the table; those for the dessert may be brought in later.

Salt and pepper, or just a pepper mill, and any other condiments or accompaniments, should be positioned centrally but to one side of the table. For a large dinner party, it is customary to have more than one set of condiments and two plates of butter. Place a butter knife near the butter.

MENU PLANNING

The success of any snack or meal, both in aesthetic and dietary terms, hinges upon the combination of food or dishes which comprise it. A few important guideline summarize the approach to planning menus for every day as well as for special occasions.

The key points to consider when planning a menu, apart from the likes and dislikes or dietary restrictions of the diners, are the flavours, textures, colour and weight of the meal. A well-planned menu balances all these elements. Additional practical aspects to consider are your ability and confidence as a cook; the budget for one meal or for a weekly – or monthly – run of meals; and the cooking facilities available.

When planning a menu, it is usual to consider the main course of the meal first, then to fit the starter, fish course or dessert around it. This does not always have to be the rule – if you have a particularly splendid starter or dessert which you want to serve at a dinner party, or even for a family meal, there is absolutely no reason why you should not work the rest of the meal around it. If, for example, you wanted to serve a chocolate fondue as the finale of a dinner party, it would be logical to keep the preceding courses light. Equally, a traditional steamed sponge pudding with custard is a real family treat but is not suitable for serving after a very filling main course, so a light salad and grilled fish would be the better option.

FLAVOURS AND TEXTURES

As well as considering the accompaniments for the main dish, remember that a strongly flavoured starter will put a lightly seasoned main course in the shade, just as a very spicy main course will ruin the palate for a delicate dessert. Balance strong flavours and aim to accentuate more subtle dishes.

Texture is a less obvious but equally important characteristic of food. A meal that consists solely of soft food is dull, and three courses of dry or crunchy dishes can be a disaster, leaving everyone gasping for water. Balance soft and smooth mixtures with crunchy textures; combine moist dishes with dry ones. Offer crisp salads with zesty dressings to counteract rich fried foods; serve plain, crunchy, lightly cooked vegetables to balance heavily-sauced casseroles and stews.

COLOUR AND WEIGHT

The importance of colour in a dish and on a menu does not simply refer to the piece of parsley dropped on to a grey sauce. The ingredients used in individual dishes, the quality of cooking juices and sauces and the choice of accompaniments are all factors in achieving a menu that looks appealing. Some cooked foods inevitably look uninteresting; this is when the choice of accompaniments is vital. Remember that flavour and texture must also be considered.

The overall weight of the meal is important. Light dishes should balance richer foods. A filling dish should always be flanked by delicate courses.

FOOD VALUE

Dinner parties and special meals are occasions for breaking or bending the rules and indulging in favourite foods. When planning everyday meals or snacks, however, it is very important to consider food value alongside the flavour, texture and appearance of the dishes. Applying rigid guidelines to every meal is not practical, but considering the overall food value of the day's diet is prudent. Taking a sensible overall view of food eaten over a period of a few days, or within a week, is also a reasonable way of ensuring that snacks and meals provide a balanced diet. From breakfast through to supper, whether considering the main meal of the day or an in-between meal snack, variety is one of the keys to success, both in the range of foods eaten and the cooking or serving methods used.

CATERING FOR SPECIAL DIETS

Be aware of any dietary restrictions for social or medical reasons, planning them into the menu for all diners as far as possible. In some cases, for example when catering for vegetarians as well as meat eaters, it is quite possible to provide one menu to suit everyone. Contemporary vegetarian dishes are acceptable to all, not simply to those who avoid animal products; it is far trickier to plan a vegan menu to suit all tastes. Limitations imposed for health reasons may be more difficult to accommodate; if in doubt, check details with the prospective guest or consult an official source of information for guidance.

If the whole menu cannot be adapted to suit everyone, plan the meal around one or two of the key dishes. It is usually quite easy to serve a first course to suit all diets. Either the main dish or vegetable accompaniments should be selected for their versatility: if the main dish is unsuitable for certain diners, then the vegetable accompaniments should make equally interesting main dishes on their own. For example, ratatouille, a mixed vegetable gratin or stir-fried vegetables with noodles are all suitable for serving with plain meat dishes but they are equally good vegetarian dishes when served with appropriate accompaniments.

Adopt this approach whenever you plan meals and snacks, but pay special attention to the food value of restricted diets if you cater for them on a regular basis. Make up for nutrients lost in banned foods by including compensatory alternatives.

PARTIES

The choice of party food depends on the number of guests and the budget – these factors influence the style of food, choice of ingredients, balance of hot and cold dishes and the number of courses. Whether you are planning a formal meal or cocktail-style buffet with snacks and nibbles, remember the following points as they are crucial to the success – or failure – of the menu.

- Time available for food preparation.
- Refrigerator space for storing ingredients and/or dishes requiring chilling.
- Kitchen facilities, particularly oven and hob space.
- Freezer space and suitability of dishes for preparing in advance.
- Availability of crockery and cutlery for serving.
- The time available for last-minute work, finishing dishes, garnishing, etc.
- Your own ability as cook – opt for a menu which you will tackle with confidence.

- Ease of serving and eating the food: the only thing worse than a host or hostess who is overstretched by last-minute cooking between courses at a formal dinner party is the poor guest who is struggling with a knife and fork while standing and balancing a plate, glass and napkin, at the same time chatting politely to other guests.

ADAPTING RECIPES

There are a number of important factors to bear in mind when catering in quantity. If you are planning to scale up a favourite recipe, first look at it carefully to see if it contains any strong flavourings. These do not need to be scaled up in the same proportions as the meat or vegetable content of the recipe, as a small amount of flavouring will penetrate quite large quantities of food. Spices, garlic, strong herbs, and proprietary sauces all need to be handled with care.

The liquid content of the dish also needs to be looked at carefully. A fish dish with sauce, for example, will not need as much sauce when produced in quantity. Stews and casseroles, too, may not need the same proportion of liquid.

Apart from the logical reasons for these differences when increasing quantities, there is also a psychological factor. When dishes are prepared for four or six people, the cook wishes the food not only to be sufficient but to look sufficient, and very often enough food is made for five or seven. Unless this factor is taken into account when scaling up, the resultant recipe for fifty would actually feed sixty or more.

APPROXIMATE QUANTITIES OF BASIC FOODS PER PERSON

Bread	*French bread:* 2 slices (with dinner; more may be eaten with salad); 3–4 slices (served with just wine and cheese) *Rolls:* 2
Butter	25 g / 1 oz
Soup	150 ml / ¼ pint
Meat	*On the bone:* 150–225 g / 5–8 oz (main course: depending on whether used in casserole with vegetables or on its own) *Off the bone:* 100–150 g / 4–5 oz (main course: depending on whether used in casserole with vegetables or on its own)

Chicken	*On the bone:* 150–225 g / 5–8 oz (main course: depending on whether used in casserole with vegetables or on its own) *Off the bone:* 100–150 g / 4–5 oz (main course: depending on whether used in casserole with vegetables or on its own)
Cheese	100 g / 4 oz (served at wine and cheese party); 50 g / 2 oz (served as last course of dinner)
Pâté	50 g / 2 oz (as first-course dish)
Fish	Fillet or steak 100–150 g / 4–5 oz (depending on whether main or subsidiary course)
Vegetables	100 g / 4 oz (served with one other vegetable and potatoes as accompaniment to main course)
Rice	25–50 g / 1–2 oz (uncooked)
Pasta	50–100 g / 2–4 oz (depending on whether main or subsidiary course)
Gravy/sauces	75–100 ml / 3–3½ fl oz (served with main dish)
Salad dressings	15–20 ml / 3–4 tsp (smaller quantity for French dressing, larger for mayonnaise)
Ice cream	50–75 ml / 2–3 fl oz (depending on richness, whether an accompaniment, etc)
Fruit	150 g / 5 oz (for fruit salad)
Pouring cream	75 ml / 3 fl oz
Tea	5 ml / 1 tsp tea leaves; 125 ml / 4 fl oz milk serves 4
Coffee	125 ml / 4 fl oz per person; 125 ml / 4 fl oz cream serves 4

For finger buffets and cocktail canapés, check by making a mental picture of one of each of all the items you are planning to serve set out together on a plate. This will give you an idea of the quantity allowed for each person.

THE CHRISTMAS COUNTDOWN

If you are catering for a number of people at Christmas, it really does pay to plan your menus and shopping in advance and prepare as much as possible. If you don't have much freezer space, consider asking friends or family to freeze elements of the feast for you. If you have a large number of people to feed, it might be worth considering hiring an extra oven (small combination ovens can simply sit on the worktop or any stable surface near a power point), or a large hot plate.

UP TO A YEAR IN ADVANCE

Christmas Pudding.
Christmas Cake – un-iced cake can be frozen – allow 4 hours to thaw.
Mincemeat – will keep chilled for 3 months, or can be frozen for a year.

UP TO THREE MONTHS IN ADVANCE

Mince Pies – 3 months if frozen cooked, 6 if uncooked.
Brandy Butter – 3 months frozen, or up to 2 weeks chilled.
Cranberry Sauce – 3 months frozen, or 2 days in advance if chilled.
Bread Sauce – 3 months frozen, 1 week chilled.

UP TO ONE MONTH IN ADVANCE

Breadcrumbs frozen for stuffing.

UP TO ONE WEEK IN ADVANCE

Thaw Christmas Cake and decorate.

FOUR DAYS IN ADVANCE

If your turkey is frozen, it will need up to 4 full days thawing in the fridge (see page 44).

CHRISTMAS EVE

Stuffing – frozen breadcrumbs will thaw very rapidly.
Prepare vegetables – keep peeled potatoes for Roast Potatoes in cold water. Brussels sprouts, carrots and parsnips can be peeled and stored in airtight bags or containers in the fridge overnight, although note that all pre-prepared vegetables lose vitamins and flavour.
Remove frozen items (bread sauce, cranberry sauce, mince pies, brandy butter, etc.) for overnight thawing in the fridge.

CHRISTMAS DAY

To serve Christmas lunch at 2.30 pm:

10 am	Remove turkey from fridge. Preheat oven at 220°C / 425°F / gas 7.
10.15 am	Stuff turkey.
10.30 am	Put turkey in oven. Prepare vegetables if not pre-prepared.
Noon	Start steaming Christmas Pudding.
1 pm	Put parsnips and potatoes on to parboil. If making own gravy, put turkey giblets and neck in pan, bring to boil, skim and simmer.

1.10 pm	Heat fat in roasting tin.
1.15 pm	Coat potatoes and parsnips in hot fat, place on top shelf of oven. Remove bacon and chipolatas from fridge.
2 pm	Check turkey is cooked through, cover with foil and a tea towel and place to rest for half an hour. Make bacon rolls / chipolata and bacon rolls and put in roasting tin in oven. Remove cranberry and bread sauce from fridge. Turn potatoes. Reheat bread sauce with milk. Put other vegetables on to boil. Warm serving dishes.
2.25 pm	Check chipolatas, bacon, potatoes and parsnips. If ready, transfer to serving dishes and keep hot. Ditto with the vegetables. Make the gravy (see page 142) and add giblet gravy to juices in roasting tin.
2.30 pm	Carve turkey and serve with stuffing.

Useful Weights and Measures

USING METRIC OR IMPERIAL MEASURES

Throughout the book, all weights and measures are given first in metric, then in imperial. For example 100 g / 4 oz, 150 ml/ ¼ pint or 15 ml / 1 tbsp.

When following any of the recipes use either metric or imperial – do not combine the two sets of measures as they are approximate equivalents, not interchangeable.

EQUIVALENT METRIC / IMPERIAL MEASURES

Weights The following chart lists some of the metric / imperial weights that are used in the recipes.

METRIC	IMPERIAL	METRIC	IMPERIAL
15 g	½ oz	375 g	13 oz
25 g	1 oz	400 g	14 oz
50 g	2 oz	425 g	15 oz
75 g	3 oz	450 g	1 lb
100 g	4 oz	575 g	1¼ lb
150 g	5 oz	675 g	1½ lb
175 g	6 oz	800 g	1¾ lb
200 g	7 oz	900 g	2 lb
225 g	8 oz	1 kg	2¼ lb
250 g	9 oz	1.4 kg	3 lb
275 g	10 oz	1.6 kg	3½ lb
300 g	11 oz	1.8 kg	4 lb
350 g	12 oz	2.25 kg	5 lb

Liquid Measures The following chart lists some metric / imperial equivalents for liquids. Millilitres (ml), litres and fluid ounces (fl oz) or pints are used throughout.

METRIC	IMPERIAL
50 ml	2 fl oz
125 ml	4 fl oz
150 ml	¼ pint
300 ml	½ pint
450 ml	¾ pint
600 ml	1 pint

Spoon Measures Both metric and imperial equivalents are given for all spoon measures, expressed as millilitres and teaspoons (tsp) or tablespoons (tbsp).

All spoon measures refer to British standard measuring spoons and the quantities given are always for level spoons.

Do not use ordinary kitchen cutlery instead of proper measuring spoons as they will hold quite different quantities.

METRIC	IMPERIAL
1.25 ml	¼ tsp
2.5 ml	½ tsp
5 ml	1 tsp
15 ml	1 tbsp

Length All linear measures are expressed in millimetres (mm), centimetres (cm) or metres (m) and inches or feet. The following list gives examples of typical conversions.

METRIC	IMPERIAL
5 mm	¼ inch
1 cm	½ inch
2.5 cm	1 inch
5 cm	2 inches
15 cm	6 inches
30 cm	12 inches (1 foot)

MICROWAVE INFORMATION

Occasional microwave hints and instructions are included for certain recipes, as appropriate. The information given is for microwave ovens rated at 650–700 watts.

The following terms have been used for the microwave settings: High, Medium, Defrost and Low. For each setting, the power input is as follows: High = 100% power, Medium = 50% power, Defrost = 30% power and Low = 20% power.

All microwave notes and timings are for guidance only: always read and follow the manufacturer's instructions for your particular appliance. Remember to avoid putting any metal in the microwave and never operate the microwave empty.

Be very careful when heating liquids in the microwave as they can 'superheat'; i.e. the liquid's surface looks still but underneath there can be boiling bubbles that explode when the container is moved.

OVEN TEMPERATURES

Whenever the oven is used, the required setting is given as three alternatives: degrees Celsius (ºC), degrees Fahrenheit (ºF) and gas.

The temperature settings given are for conventional ovens. If you have a fan oven, adjust the temperature according to the manufacturer's instructions.

ºC	ºF	GAS
110	225	¼
120	250	½
140	275	1
150	300	2
160	325	3
180	350	4
190	375	5
200	400	6
220	425	7
230	450	8
240	475	9

Index

adapting recipes 237
alcohol
  Bananas in Rum 165
  Bishop 226
  Brandy and Almond Butter 196
  Brandy Butter 194
  Brandy Snaps 212
  Carrots with Cider 112
  Cider Syllabub 169
  Claret and Lemonade Cooler 227
  Classic Liqueur Custard 190
  Curaçao and Claret Cup 227
  Fruit Claret Cup 227
  Home-made Noyeau 230
  Liqueur Sauce 186
  Mulled Ale 225
  Mulled Cider 226
  Mulled Wine 225
  Mushrooms in Bacon and Wine 123
  Orange Brandy 229
  Orange Liqueur Butter 195
  Pears in Wine 164–5
  Pineapple and Kirsch Salad 163
  Plums with Port 166
  Port Wine Jelly 168
  Rum and Brandy Toddy 228
  Sherry Butter 194
  Whisky Punch 228
  White Wine Fish Stock 19
  Wine Syllabub 168–9
Alcohol-free Punch 224
Ale, Mulled 225
Almond Paste 200
Angels on Horseback 33
Anna Potatoes 107
appetizers 32–8
  Angels on Horseback 33
  Burlington Croûtes 34
  Cheese Butterflies 37
  Gravad Lax 32
  Hot Pepper Cheeses 36
  Mrs Beeton's Cheese Straws 35
  Mrs Beeton's Pastry Ramekins 34–5
  Saucy Angels 33
  Spicy Nuts 38
apples
  Apple and Celery Stuffing 133
  Apple and Ginger Cake 207
  Apple Crumble 175
  Apple Sauce 148
  Baked Apples 177
  Baked Apples Stuffed with Rice and Nuts 178
  Brown Apple Sauce 148
  Brown Betty 176
  Cranberry and Apple Jelly 146
  Frosted Apples 170–1
  Panfried Onion and Apple 119
  Prune and Apple Stuffing 138
  Roast Goose with Apples and Onions 52–3
  Roast Venison with Baked Apples 70
apricots
  Apricot Glaze 199
  Apricot Stuffing 137

bacon
  Bacon Rolls 47
  Mushrooms in Bacon and Wine 123
Baked Apples 177
Baked Apples Stuffed with Rice and Nuts 178
Baked Ham Loaf 89
Baked Soup 11
Bananas in Rum 165
Barbecue Sauce 49
Bavarian Cabbage 126
beans
  Bean Soup 8
  Boston Roast 101
  Soya Bean Bake 104
  Two-Bean Soup 8
  Vegetarian Bean Soup 8
Béarnaise Sauce 153
Béchamel Sauce 154
beef
  Baked Soup 11
  Beef Wellington 74–5
  Carbonnade of Beef 76–7
  Châteaubriand Steak 77
  Meatloaf 90
  Potted Beef 24–5
  Roast Ribs of Beef with Yorkshire Pudding 72–3
Beurre Manié (Mrs Beeton's Tip) 79
Bishop 226
Black Forest Gâteau 208–9
Bombe Tortoni 182
Borsch 2
Boston Roast 101
Braised Chestnut Chicken 56–7
Braised Chestnuts with Onion and Celery 125
brandy
  Brandy and Almond Butter 196
  Brandy Butter 194
  Brandy Snaps 212
  Orange Brandy 229
  Rum and Brandy Toddy 228
Bread and Butter Pudding 179
Bread Sauce 144
breadcrumbs (Mrs Beeton's Tips) 121, 140
Brown Apple Sauce 148
Brown Betty 176
brussels sprouts 110
  Brussels Sprouts with Chestnuts 110
Bûche de Nöel 206–7
buffets 232
Burlington Croûtes 34
Buttered Leeks 113
butters
  Beurre Manié (Mrs Beeton's Tip) 79
  Brandy and Almond Butter 196
  Brandy Butter 194
  Chestnut Butter 196
  Clarified Butter 23
  Lemon Butter 194

Maître d'Hôtel Butter
Orange Butter 194
Orange Liqueur Butter 195
quantities 237
Sherry Butter 194
Sweet Butters 194
Vanilla Butter 194

cabbage
Bavarian Cabbage 126
Cabbage Soup 6
Duck and Red Cabbage 59
Red Cabbage 54
Roast Goose with Fruit Stuffing and Red Cabbage 54–5
Sauerkraut with Juniper Berries 127
Candied Peel, Quick 220
Caramel 191
Carbonnade of Beef 76–7
carrots
Carrot and Orange Soup 7
Carrot Soup 7
Carrots with Cider 112
Glazed Carrots 111
microwave cooking (Mrs Beeton's Tip) 112
catering for special diets 236
cauliflower
Cauliflower Cheese 114–5
Cauliflower Polonaise 115
Cauliflower Soup 9
celeriac
Celeriac and Potato Purée 117
Celeriac Purée 117
microwave cooking (Mrs Beeton's Tip) 117
celery
Apple and Celery Stuffing 133
Braised Chestnuts with Onion and Celery 125
Châteaubriand Steak 77
cheese
Cauliflower Cheese 114–5
Cheese Butterflies 37
Gratin Dauphinois 108
Hot Pepper Cheeses 36
Lentil and Stilton Lasagne 102
Mrs Beeton's Cheese Straws 35
Mrs Beeton's Pastry Ramekins 34–5
planning a cheese course 183–4
quantities 238
Swiss Cheese Fondue 103
chestnuts
Braised Chestnut Chicken 56–7
Braised Chestnuts with Onion and Celery 125
Bûche de Nöel (Chestnut Christmas Log) 206–7
Chestnut and Ham Stuffing 56
Chestnut and Onion Stuffing 132
Chestnut Butter 196
Chestnut Sauce 145
Chestnut Soup 3
Chestnut Stuffing 46, 131
preparing (Mrs Beeton's Tip) 132
Roast Turkey with Chestnuts 46–7
roasting 38
shelling (Mrs Beeton's Tip) 3, 111
chicken
Braised Chestnut Chicken 56–7
Burlington Croûtes 34
Chicken Mousse 31
Chicken Stock 18
Cock-a-Leekie 14
quantities 238
Rich Chicken Stock 19
Roast Chicken with Honey and Almonds 55
roasting times 42
see also poultry
chocolate
Chocolate Cream Sauce 192
Chocolate Custard Sauce 186
Chocolate-tipped Cinnamon Stars 214
Christmas Cake 198–202
Almond Paste 200
applying icing 202
Apricot Glaze 199
decorating 199
Royal Icing 201
Christmas countdown 239–41
Christmas Pudding
flaming (Mrs Beeton's Tip) 159
Plum Pudding 158–9
pressure cooking 157
Rich Christmas Pudding 156–7
storing 157
Vegetarian Plum Pudding 160
Christmas Stöllen 204–5
Christopher North's Sauce 150
cider
Carrots with Cider 112
Cider Syllabub 169
Cinnamon Bars 210
Citrus Glazed Onions 120
Claret and Lemonade Cooler 227
Clarified Butter 23
Classic Egg Custard Sauce 190
Classic Lemon Custard 190
Classic Liqueur Custard 190
Classic Orange Custard 190
Cock-a-Leekie 14
condiments 234
Cornflour Custard Sauce 187
Courgettes with Almonds 116
Court Bouillon 92
cranberries
Cranberry and Apple Jelly 146
Cranberry Raisin Pie 217
Cranberry Sauce 146
Cream Custard Sauce 188
Creamed Onions 121
Crème Anglaise 186
Crown Roast of Lamb 82
Cumberland sauce 147
Curaçao and Claret Cup 227
cutlery 234

Devilled Turkey 49
Dried Fruit Compote 172
Duchesse Potatoes 106–7
duck
Duck and Red Cabbage 59
English Roast Duck 58
roasting times 42
see also poultry

English Roast Duck 58
Excellent Mincemeat 218

Fennel with Leeks 118
fish and seafood 92–8
Angels on Horseback 33
Fish Stock 19
French Fried Haddock 98
Gravad Lax 32

Herbed Herring Roe Pâté 27
Herring Roe and Prawn Pâté 27
Herring Roe Pâté 27
Herring Roe Sauce 27
Hot Poached Salmon 92–4
Kedgeree 95
Koulibiac 96–7
Potted Salmon 22
Potted Shrimps or Prawns 22
quantities 238
Saucy Angels 33
Smoked Haddock Chowder 12
Smoked Mackerel Pâté 26
White Wine Fish Stock 19
Flaky Pastry 221
fleurons (Mrs Beeton's Tip) 125
Florentines 211
food quantities 237–8
food value 235
Forcemeat *see* Mrs Beeton's Forcemeat
French Fried Haddock 98
Frosted Apples 170–1
Fruit Claret Cup 227

game 64–70
Game Stock 19
Guineafowl with Grapes 65
Normandy Partridges 66
Orange-scented Braised Venison 68–9
Pheasant with Mushroom Stuffing 67
Potted Game 25
Potted Venison 24
Roast Guineafowl 64
Roast Venison with Baked Apples 70
German Spice Biscuits 213
Ginger
Apple and Ginger Cake 207
Ginger Pudding 161
Ginger Syrup Sauce 193
Rich Gingerbread 209
Glazed Carrots 111
Glazed Onions 120
goose
Roast Goose with Apples and Onions 52–3
Roast Goose with Fruit Stuffing and Red Cabbage 54–5
roasting times 42
see also poultry
Gratin Dauphinois 108
Gravad Lax 32
Gravy 142–3
Guard of Honour 82
guineafowl
Guineafowl with Grapes 65
Roast Guineafowl 64

haddock
French Fried Haddock 98
Kedgeree 95
Smoked Haddock Chowder 12
ham
Baked Ham Loaf 89
Honey-Glazed Ham 88
Marmalade-Glazed Ham 89
Hashed Turkey 48
herbs
Herb Forcemeat 46
Herb Stuffing 134
Herbed Herring Roe Pâté 27
Herbed Shoulder of Lamb 78–9
Lemon and Herb Stuffing 135
Lemon and Parsley Stuffing 80–1
Sage and Onion Stuffing 136
herring
Herbed Herring Roe Pâté 27
Herring Roe and Prawn Pâté 27
Herring Roe Pâté 27
Herring Roe Sauce 27
Hollandaise Sauce 152–3
Home-made Noyeau 230
honey
Honey-Glazed Ham 88
Roast Chicken with Honey and Almonds 55
Horseradish Sauce 150
Hot Pepper Cheeses 36
Hot Poached Salmon 92–4

Italian Spinach 118–9

Japanese Plombière 180–1
Jerusalem Artichoke Soup 4

Kedgeree 95
Koulibiac 96–7
lamb
Baked Soup 11
Crown Roast of Lamb 82
Guard of Honour 82
Herbed Shoulder of Lamb 78–9
Lamb Cutlets en Papillote 83
Loin of Lamb with Lemon and Parsley Stuffing 80–1
Roast Rack of Lamb 82
Scotch Broth 15
leeks
Buttered Leeks 113
Cock-a-Leekie 14
Fennel with Leeks 118
Lentil and Leek Lasagne 103
washing leeks (Mrs Beeton's Tip) 113
Leftover Turkey 48
lemons 45 (Mrs Beeton's Tip)
Classic Lemon Custard 190
Lemon and Herb Stuffing 135
Lemon and Parsley Stuffing 80–1
Lemon Butter 194
Lemon Mincemeat 219
lentils
Lentil and Leek Lasagne 103
Lentil and Stilton Lasagne 102
liqueurs
Classic Liqueur Custard 190
Curaçao and Claret Cup 227
Liqueur Sauce 186
Orange Liqueur Butter 195
Pineapple and Kirsch Salad 163
Liver Pâté 28–9
Loin of Lamb with Lemon and Parsley Stuffing 80–1
Loin of Pork Stuffed with Prunes 85

mackerel
Smoked Mackerel Pâté 26
Maître d'Hôtel Butter
Marmalade-Glazed Ham 89
Meatloaf 90
menu planning 234
adapting recipes 237

catering for special diets 236
food quantities 237–8
food value 235
parties 236
Mince Pies 215
mincemeat
Cranberry Raisin Pie 217
Excellent Mincemeat 218
Lemon Mincemeat 219
Mince Pies 215
Mincemeat Meringue Pie 216
Mrs Beeton's Cheese Straws 35
Mrs Beeton's Forcemeat 139
Mrs Beeton's Forcemeat Balls 139
Mrs Beeton's Orange Salad 164
Mrs Beeton's Pastry Ramekins 34–5
Mrs Beeton's Roast Turkey 45
Mrs Beeton's Trifle 162–3
Mulled Ale 225
Mulled Cider 226
Mulled Wine 225
mushrooms
Mushroom and Corn Stuffing 84–5
Mushroom Stuffing 67, 140
Mushrooms in Bacon and Wine 123
Mushrooms in Cream Sauce 122
storing (Mrs Beeton's Tip) 123
Stuffed Mushrooms 124
mussels
Saucy Angels 33
Mustard Sauce 32

Normandy Partridges 66
Noyeau, Home-made 230
Nutty Plum Crumble 174
nuts
Baked Apples Stuffed with Rice and Nuts 178
Brandy and Almond Butter 196
Nut Roast 100
Nutty Plum Crumble 174
Roast Chicken with Honey and Almonds 55
Spicy Nuts 38
Walnut Stuffing 135

onions
Braised Chestnuts with Onion and Celery 125
Chestnut and Onion Stuffing 132
Citrus Glazed Onions 120
Creamed Onions 121
Glazed Onions 120
Panfried Onion and Apple 119
Sage and Onion Stuffing 136
Scalloped Potatoes with Onions 108–9
oranges
Carrot and Orange Soup 7
Classic Orange Custard 190
Mrs Beeton's Orange Salad 164
Orange Brandy 229
Orange Butter 194
Orange Liqueur Butter 195
Oranges in Caramel Sauce 167
Orange-scented Braised Venison 68–9
oysters
Angels on Horseback 33

Panfried Onion and Apple 119
parsnips
Parsnip Soup 5
Roast Parsnips 109
Spiced Parsnip Soup 5
parties 236
partridge
Normandy Partridges 66
pastry
Cheese Butterflies 37
Cranberry Raisin Pie 217
Flaky Pastry 221
fleurons (Mrs Beeton's Tip) 125
Hot Pepper Cheeses 36
Mince Pies 215
Mincemeat Meringue Pie 216
Mrs Beeton's Cheese Straws 35
Mrs Beeton's Pastry Ramekins 34–5
Puff Pastry 74–5
Rough Puff Pastry 222
Short Crust Pastry 215, 216, 217
tips for success 222

pâtés and mousses 22–31
Chicken or Turkey Mousse 31
Herbed Herring Roe Pâté 27
Herring Roe and Prawn Pâté 27
Herring Roe Pâté 27
Liver Pâté 28–9
Pâté Maison 30
Potted Beef 24–5
Potted Game 25
Potted Ham 23
Potted Salmon 22
Potted Shrimps or Prawns 22
Potted Venison 24
quantities 238
Smoked Mackerel Pâté 26
peas
Pea and Ham Soup 10
Pease Pudding 128
Poultry with Peas 60
Yellow Split Pea Soup 10
Pears in Wine 164–5
Pease Pudding 128
Petits Pois à la Française 116
Pheasant with Mushroom Stuffing 67
Pineapple and Kirsch Salad 163
place settings 232
alternative settings 233
formal settings 233
plombières
Japanese Plombière 180–1
Vanilla Plombière 180–1
Plum Pudding 158–9
Plum Pudding Sauce 191
plums
Nutty Plum Crumble 174
Plums with Port 166
pork
Liver Pâté 28–9
Loin of Pork Stuffed with Prunes 85
Meatloaf 90
Mrs Beeton's Forcemeat 139
Mrs Beeton's Forcemeat Balls 139
Pâté Maison 30
Roast Pork with Mushroom and Corn Stuffing 84–5
Roast Pork with Sage and Onion Stuffing 87

Sausagemeat Stuffing 138
Savoury Loin of Pork 86
Port Wine Jelly 168
potatoes
Anna Potatoes 107
Celeriac and Potato Purée 117
Duchesse Potatoes 106–7
Gratin Dauphinois 108
Roast Potatoes 106
Scalloped Potatoes with Onions 108–9
Potted Beef 24–5
Potted Game 25
Potted Ham 23
Potted Salmon 22
Potted Shrimps or Prawns 22
Potted Venison 24
poultry 40–63
boning 41
Braised Chestnut Chicken 56–7
Burlington Croûtes 34
carving 43
Chicken or Turkey Mousse 31
Chicken Stock 18
Cock-a-Leekie 14
Devilled Turkey 49
Duck and Red Cabbage 59
English Roast Duck 58
freezing 4
Hashed Turkey 48
jointing 41
Leftover Turkey 48
Mrs Beeton's Roast Turkey 45
Poultry à la Béchamel 62
Poultry Fritters 63
Poultry Pilau 61
Poultry with Peas 60
preparing 40
Rich Chicken Stock 19
Roast Chicken with Honey and Almonds 55
Roast Goose with Apples and Onions 52–3
Roast Goose with Fruit Stuffing and Red Cabbage 54–5
Roast Turkey with Chestnuts 46–7
roasting times 42
spatchcock 41
stuffing 40
testing 43
thawing 44
Turkey and Chipolata Hotpot 50
Turkey Croquettes 48
Turkey Loaf 51
Turkey Soup 13
prawns
Potted Shrimps or Prawns 22
prunes
Prune and Apple Stuffing 138
Prune Sauce 149
Puff Pastry 74–5

Red Cabbage 54
rhubarb
Spiced Rhubarb Cobbler 173
rice
Baked Apples Stuffed with Rice and Nuts 178
Kedgeree 95
Poultry Pilau 61
quantities 238
Wild Rice Stuffing 136–7
Rich Chicken Stock 19
Rich Christmas Pudding 156–7
Rich Gingerbread 209
Rich Strong Stock 16
Roast Chicken with Honey and Almonds 55
Roast Goose with Apples and Onions 52–3
Roast Goose with Fruit Stuffing and Red Cabbage 54–5
Roast Guineafowl 64
Roast Parsnips 109
Roast Pork with Mushroom and Corn Stuffing 84–5
Roast Pork with Sage and Onion Stuffing 87
Roast Potatoes 106
Roast Rack of Lamb 82
Roast Ribs of Beef with Yorkshire Pudding 72–3
Roast Turkey with Chestnuts 46–7
Roast Venison with Baked Apples 70
Rough Puff Pastry 222
Royal Icing 201
rum
Bananas in Rum 165
Rum and Brandy Toddy 228
Sage and Onion Stuffing 136
salmon
boning 93
dressing 93
garnishing 94
Gravad Lax 32
Hot Poached Salmon 92–4
Koulibiac 96–7
Potted Salmon 22
servings from salmon 93
sauces, savoury 142–54
Apple Sauce 148
Barbecue Sauce 49
Béarnaise Sauce 153
Béchamel Sauce 154
Bread Sauce 144
Brown Apple Sauce 148
Chestnut Sauce 145
Christopher North's Sauce 150
Cranberry and Apple Jelly 146
Cranberry Sauce 146
Cumberland sauce 147
Gravy 142–3
Herring Roe Sauce 27
Hollandaise Sauce 152–3
Horseradish Sauce 150
Maître d'Hôtel Butter
Mustard Sauce 32
Prune Sauce 149
quantities 238
Tomato Sauce 151
sauces, sweet 186–93
Caramel 191
Chocolate Cream Sauce 192
Chocolate Custard Sauce 186
Classic Egg Custard Sauce 190
Classic Lemon Custard 190
Classic Liqueur Custard 190
Classic Orange Custard 190
Cornflour Custard Sauce 187
Cream Custard Sauce 188
Crème Anglaise 186
Ginger Syrup Sauce 193
Liqueur Sauce 186
Plum Pudding Sauce 191
Simple Custard Sauce 189
Vanilla Custard 188–9
Saucy Angels 33

Sauerkraut with Juniper Berries 127
Sausagemeat Stuffing 138
Savoury Loin of Pork 86
Scalloped Potatoes with Onions 108–9
Scotch Broth 15
Sherry Butter 194
Short Crust Pastry 215, 216, 217
Simple Custard Sauce 189
Smoked Haddock Chowder 12
Smoked Mackerel Pâté 26
soups 2–15
  Baked Soup 11
  Bean Soup 8
  Borsch 2
  Cabbage Soup 6
  Carrot and Orange Soup 7
  Carrot Soup 7
  Cauliflower Soup 9
  Chestnut Soup 3
  Cock-a-Leekie 14
  Jerusalem Artichoke Soup 4
  Parsnip Soup 5
  Pea and Ham Soup 10
  quantites 237
  Scotch Broth 15
  Smoked Haddock Chowder 12
  Spiced Parsnip Soup 5
  Turkey Soup 13
  Two-Bean Soup 8
  Vegetarian Bean Soup 8
  Yellow Split Pea Soup 10
Soya Bean Bake 104
Spiced Parsnip Soup 5
Spiced Rhubarb Cobbler 173
Spicy Nuts 38
spinach
  Italian Spinach 118–9
spirits *see* alcohol
stocks 16–20
  Chicken Stock 18
  clarifying stock 17
  Court Bouillon 92
  Fish Stock 19
  Game Stock 19
  pressure cooking 17
  Rich Chicken Stock 19
  Rich Strong Stock 16
  Vegetable Stock 20
  White Stock 18
  White Wine Fish Stock 19
Stöllen *see* Christmas Stöllen
Stuffed Mushrooms 124
stuffings 130–40
  Apple and Celery Stuffing 133
  Apricot Stuffing 137
  Chestnut and Ham Stuffing 56
  Chestnut and Onion Stuffing 132
  Chestnut Stuffing 46, 131
  Herb Forcemeat 46
  Herb Stuffing 134
  Lemon and Herb Stuffing 135
  Lemon and Parsley Stuffing 80–1
  Mrs Beeton's Forcemeat 139
  Mrs Beeton's Forcemeat Balls 139
  Mushroom and Corn Stuffing 84–5
  Mushroom Stuffing 67, 140
  Prune and Apple Stuffing 138
  Sage and Onion Stuffing 136
  Sausagemeat Stuffing 138
  stuffing balls (Mrs Beeton's Tip) 134
  Walnut Stuffing 135
  Wild Rice Stuffing 136–7
Sweet Butters 194
Swiss Cheese Fondue 103
syllabubs
  Cider Syllabub 169
  Wine Syllabub 168–9

table laying 232
  alternative settings 233
  buffets 232
  condiments 234
  cutlery 234
  formal settings 233
  place settings 232
  table decorations 232
Tomato Sauce 151
Trifle *see* Mrs Beeton's Trifle
turkey
  Burlington Croûtes 34
  Devilled Turkey 49
  Hashed Turkey 48
  Leftover Turkey 48
  Mrs Beeton's Roast Turkey 45
  Roast Turkey with Chestnuts 46–7
  roasting times 43
  thawing times 44
  Turkey and Chipolata Hotpot 50
  Turkey Croquettes 48
  Turkey Loaf 51
  Turkey Mousse 31
  Turkey Soup 13
  see also poultry
Twelfth Night Cake 203
Two-Bean Soup 8

Vanilla Butter 194
Vanilla Custard 188–9
Vanilla Plombière 180–1
Vegetable Stock 20
Vegetarian Bean Soup 8
Vegetarian Mincemeat 220
Vegetarian Plum Pudding 160
venison
  Orange-scented Braised Venison 68–9
  Potted Venison 24
  Roast Venison with Baked Apples 70

Walnut Stuffing 135
whisky
  Home-made Noyeau 230
  Whisky Punch 228
White Stock 18
White Wine Fish Stock 19
Wild Rice Stuffing 136–7
Wine Syllabub 168–9
wine
  Bishop 226
  Claret and Lemonade Cooler 227
  Curaçao and Claret Cup 227
  Fruit Claret Cup 227
  Mulled Wine 225
  Mushrooms in Bacon and Wine 123
  Pears in Wine 164–5
  Plums with Port 166
  Port Wine Jelly 168
  Sherry Butter 194
  White Wine Fish Stock 19
  Wine Syllabub 168–9

Yellow Split Pea Soup 10
Yorkshire Pudding 72–3